BABYLON HEIGHTS

Dean Cavanagh lives in Bradford, West Yorkshire,
with his wife and children.

Irvine Welsh is the author of eight books of fiction
and one play.

ALSO BY IRVINE WELSH

Fiction

Trainspotting

The Acid House

Marabou Stork Nightmares

Ecstasy

Filth

Glue

Porno

The Bedroom Secrets of the Master Chefs

Drama

You'll Have Had Your Hole

Screenplay

The Acid House

IRVINE WELSH
AND
DEAN CAVANAGH

Babylon
Heights

VINTAGE BOOKS
London

Published by Vintage 2006

2 4 6 8 10 9 7 5 3 1

First published in Great Britain in 2006 by Vintage

Vintage
Random House, 20 Vauxhall Bridge Road,
London SW1V 2SA

Random House Australia (Pty) Limited
20 Alfred Street, Milsons Point, Sydney,
New South Wales 2061, Australia

Random House New Zealand Limited
18 Poland Road, Glenfield, Auckland 10, New Zealand

Random House (Pty) Limited
Isle of Houghton, Corner of Boundary Road & Carse O'Gowrie,
Houghton, 2198, South Africa

The Random House Group Limited Reg. No. 954009
www.randomhouse.co.uk/vintage

A CIP catalogue record for this book
is available from the British Library

ISBN 9780099505983 (from Jan 2007)
ISBN 0099505983

Papers used by Random House are natural, recyclable products
made from wood grown in sustainable forests. The manufacturing
processes conform to the environmental regulations of the
country of origin

Printed and bound in Great Britain by
Cox & Wyman Ltd, Reading, Berkshire

Introduction

In 1935, in depression America, MGM studios in Hollywood embarked on a major film project: a movie adaptation of L. Frank Baum's book *The Wonderful Wizard of Oz*. The resulting film not only lived up to the old cliché of becoming a timeless cinematic classic, it also propelled the first modern fable from America into the popular universal cultural heritage, putting Oz-lore alongside the likes of Lewis Carroll's *Alice's Adventures in Wonderland*.

The production was highly ambitious; among other things, it called for the casting of many dwarfs, who would play the little people of the mythical land of Oz, the Munchkins. The studio began the recruitment of the small persons, not just from all corners of the USA, but from all over the world.

This mass importation of dwarfs into Hollywood was not always the delightful, benevolent and painless process as suggested by the optimistic and uplifting movie. In keeping with the uninformed spirit of discrimination that prevailed against visibly different people back in those days, all the dwarf performers were billeted in the Culver Hotel, separate from the rest of the cast and crew.

Once settled, the small performers behaved in much the same way any other group of people leaving home to work on an exciting new project would. Rumours persisted of wild Munchkin parties and drunken behaviour. Judy Garland herself made reference to this in 1967, disparaging the dwarf performers as 'little drunks' on live television. The plethora of official and fan-based literature growing up around *The Wizard of Oz* has generally sought to play this down, usually dismissing the remark as 'a joke'.

However, Garland's hints of dwarf debauchery merely echoed comments made by the film's producer Mervyn LeRoy. At the time of the motion picture's release, he also 'joked' of Munchkin sex orgies and police regularly being called to the hotel. Interestingly, Judy Garland's daughters would later echo their mother's claims.

Clearly, given the nature of any Hollywood production, the time people spend away from their homes on demanding film sets and stuck in claustrophobic hotel rooms, the absence of the rowdy excesses often associated with the film industry would be rather peculiar.

More sinisterly, the macabre assertion that a Munchkin committed suicide by hanging himself on the set, during filming, has become a persistent Hollywood myth. This is said to be visible in the final print of the movie, supposedly at the Tin Man scene, where what certainly looks like a small human body is clearly visible hanging from a tree. Official sources have disparaged this contention, claiming that this figure was simply a bird. We'll probably never find out what actually happened, but imagine that a Munchkin did indeed hang himself. What could have possibly driven him to such a desperate act?

Babylon Heights

This play is dedicated to the memory of Julia De Vittoris (1965–2001) whose 'lust for life' was second to none.

'Even giants get lost in Hollywood.'
Bert Kowalski

Babylon Heights premiered at the Exit Theatre, San Francisco, on 14 June 2006.

This play benefited greatly from read-throughs at the Magic Theatre and the Edinburgh Castle in San Francisco and the Attic Studios in Dublin. Special thanks to Alan Black, Jim Reece, Jessica Heidt, Beth Quinn, Emer Martin, Graham Cantwell and Rachel Rath.

Characters

Bert Kowalski, *mid-forties, born in New Jersey, grew up in poverty, he has spent most of his adult life performing in circuses and freak shows. As a result he has formed a harsh view of performing dwarf life, basically believing that it is undignified humiliation for money. His cynical, wise-guy behaviour is his defence against the harsh world.*

Bert's dwarfism probably comes from non-genetic causes: chronic kidney diseases, diseases where the body doesn't absorb protein normally (cystic fibrosis etc.), malnutrition in early life or heart and lung disease.

Charles Merryweather, *early twenties, born in Streatham, London, he comes from a middle-class family. His father was a doctor who was guilty of not recognising that his son suffered from Turner's syndrome. As well as restricted growth, Turner's syndrome sufferers are also characterised by diminished or absent sex glands and no puberty. Thus Charles has little concept of sex or sexuality. His voice is quite high and he will look like a young boy.*

His early life was largely innocent and idyllic, spent playing, often alone, in the large family garden, which gave him a love of nature. He went on to find employment as a gardener at Kew Gardens, his life in the workforce a far harsher experience.

Raymond Benedict-Porter, *late forties, born in Vermont, he comes from a well-to-do New England family. Although he has done the same 'dwarf circuit' as Bert, Raymond has always had serious thespian ambitions. He probably suffers from chondrodystrophy, a form of dwarfism believed to be hereditary.*

Like many such affected persons, Raymond is physically very strong and dexterous. He has a high self-regard, seeing himself as an actor, whose height is almost an irrelevant factor. When he does acknowledge his condition, he is more likely to look to artistic dwarfs like nineteenth-century French painter Toulouse-Lautrec for inspiration, rather than to his peers.

Philomena Kinsella, *mid-twenties, born in County Kerry, Ireland, she probably suffers from pituitary dwarfism, which is caused by the body producing insufficient growth hormones. In the present day, like many other forms of the condition, this has been all but wiped out. With pituitary dwarfism, the sufferer's proportions are normal and they tend to* *have a doll-like appearance and are often possessed with above average intelligence.*

Philomena comes from a remote and rural part of Ireland, where old myths regarding the 'little people' still held sway at the turn of the last century. Irish leprechauns are associated with trees and bushes and some peasant people who have had a dwarf child believe it is their duty to 'give them to the little people' i.e. leave them in the woods for other leprechauns to look after.

The requirement to lead this kind of subsistence life is probably why leprechauns have the association with mischief, trickery and deviousness. Like many of them, Philomena would have needed to steal and con, usually from local farmers, simply in order to survive.

Settings

Act One, Scene One: 1930s hotel room in Culver City, California.

Act One, Scene Two: a restaurant dining room in Culver City.

Act Two: 1930s hotel room in Culver City, California.

Staging Notes

In order to maximise audience empathy with the 'trapped' dwarfs, the four actors who play the Munchkins will be of 'regular' size. Instead, the stage equipment – beds, doors, table, etc. – will be outsized. The production is best suited to a small space, probably a 'black box' stage, which should feel tight and claustrophobic, where the audience will be very close to the production.

The only reference to the outside world is the booming offstage voice of the 'normal people', which should be intrusive and threatening.

Act One

Scene One

We hear the strains of the song 'The Wonderful Wizard of Oz' and the lights go up on a mid-1930s hotel room. There are four beds, four chairs, a dressing table, mirror on the wall, a sink, a wardrobe, a chest of drawers with a telephone on top, a door rear centre-stage and one to the left leading to a bathroom. A set of Hotel Regulations is posted on the wall.

Everything is outsized; the beds are twelve-foot long and eight-foot wide, and the door is at least twelve-foot high.

Bert *– New Jersey accent, forties, shabbily suited, with a permanent scowl etched on to his face, carrying a battered outsized suitcase – pushes the door open and stands at the threshold looking in.*

As the music fades we hear a voice offstage.

Booming male voice (*off*)   There you go, shorty. Make the most of it. (*Laughter.*)

Bert *looks up in the direction of the voice, glares, steps in and shuts the door behind him.* **Bert** *is forever wiping sweat from his brow with a handkerchief.*

Bert   Cocksucker!

He sighs, puts down his case and explores the room. He views it with disdain.

. . . cheap lousy cocksucken...

He coughs loudly and climbs up on to the bed and begins to jump up and down on it as he starts to undress. As he is trying to take off one of his shoes he falters, staggers and falls off the bed, crashing to the floor.

(*Clambering to his feet.*) Fuck!

Going to his case, **Bert** *sits down on it and lights a cigarette (three times the regular size). He looks around the room and shakes his head. He pulls the sleeve of his jacket back to reveal his watch. It is three times the* *regular size of a watch. He reads it and pulls the sleeve back over it. He stares out at us for a while, smoking, then gets up and opens his case. He pulls out a script (three times the regular size), sits back down and flicks through it.*

. . . shit. Piece o' goddam shit . . .

He coughs again and goes to the chair, puts it in position, climbs up and picks up the phone.

. . . that the desk? . . . yeah, Michigan . . . uh? . . . yeah, yeah, I hear ya . . . OK, OK . . . fuck you very much, OK . . . yeah, that's right, you heard me right, honey: fuck you very much, OK.

He slams the phone on the hook and climbs down.

Asshole!

He goes back to his case, picks it up and takes it over to the chest of drawers. He opens the bottom drawer and starts to put his clothes in.

The door opens and **Charles** *– English, early twenties, nervous, suited, carrying a case – enters. He puts his case down and surveys the room. He is clearly impressed with it.*

Bert   Don't even *think* about calling out.

Charles   Calling out?

Bert   Lousy studio cocksuckers.

Charles   Ah . . .

Bert   Sucks you ask me, kid.

Charles *heads over to* **Bert***.*

Charles *(extending his hand)*   Charles Merryweather, London, England.

Bert *glances at* **Charles***'s hand and carries on putting his clothes away.*

Bert   Bert Kowalski, no fixed abode.

Charles *waits, then awkwardly rubs his hands against his trousers and explores the room.*

Charles   . . . Culver Heights, the name alone – smashing. The grounds – so beautiful! The flora and fauna, those gorgeous palm trees! You think they might have some picture postcards for sale?

Bert   Picture postcards?

Charles   To send home.

Bert   You one of Singer's?

Charles   I didn't know I would have to sing –

Bert   No, Singer's mob, Leo Singer, the schmuck who got the MGM contract to recruit the likes of us.

Charles   Ah, yes.

Bert *closes the drawer and climbs up on the bed.*

Bert *(delving into his pocket)*   You smoke?

Charles   That's very kind.

Bert *pulls out a lighter and waits.*

Bert   . . . Well?

Charles *cottons on.*

Charles   Oh, right, I see.

Charles *pulls out a cigarette case and offers it up to* **Bert**. **Bert** *has to reach down to take a cigarette.*

Bert *(lighting it up)*   I heard somewhere cigarettes stunt your growth.

Charles   Oh?

Bert   I don't listen to gossip though.

Charles *frowns and lights his cigarette.*

Bert   So, they've got midgets in England then, uh?

Charles (*affronted*)   Midgets?

Bert   English, right?

Charles   You said –

Bert *points to himself and* **Charles**.

Bert   Dwarfs, leprechauns, Munchkins, little people . . .
freaks. You know, fucken *midgets*.

Charles *sighs and goes to his case. He picks it up and heads over to
the chest of drawers.*

Bert (*watching* **Charles** *put his clothes away*)   You read the
storyplay yet?

Charles   The story, yes, I've –

Bert   What you think?

Charles   I think it's very well written.

Bert   That mean you *like it?*

Charles   Yes, yes, I wouldn't be out here if I didn't believe
it had artistic merit.

Bert *laughs and lies back on the bed.* **Charles** *sighs and continues
putting his belongings away.*

Charles   Have I said something funny?

Bert   . . . *artistic merit?*

Charles   Well, yes, yes, it's very –

Bert   It ain't your fucken Shakespeare, right? Alas, poor
Tin Woodsman, I knew him well. Piece o' sophomore shit
you ask me. You ask me it's a fucken waste o' time piece o'
shit.

Charles   I must, really, I mean, I must say I find your
language . . . well . . .

Bert   Yeah?

Charles   I . . . I don't want us to get off on the wrong foot
here.

Bert   *Wrong foot?* What're you trying – spit it out, uh, just
spit it, OK.

Charles   . . . Well . . . well, what I mean is, I mean I'm
unused to it.

Bert   American? You're not – you're *unused* to the
American language, you don't understand me, right? That it,
Charlie? You don't understand me?

Charles   No, I mean, I mean yes I understand you, I
understand, it's just, don't take this the wrong way.

Bert   I won't, what is it, what're you trying to say? You
wanna spit it out for me?

Charles   I find it very coarse.

Bert   American?

Charles   I don't –

Bert   You find *American* coarse?

Charles (*closing the drawer*)   Yes, I mean, no, I mean –

Bert   Sounds to me you don't know what you mean.

Charles   It's the . . . you know, the – must you use
vulgarities?

Bert   Like *midget?* You mean like midget, right?

Charles *fingers his temples, exasperated. He takes a deep breath. He
goes to the bed and looks up at* **Bert**.

Charles   I think we've got off on the wrong foot here.
We're going to be spending a lot of time together and I, I
think it only right and proper that we try to get along. I'm just
not, I mean, I find it very . . . well, it's very off – its off-
putting.

Bert *laughs at* **Charles**.

Bert . . . I'm fucken shitting you, kid. I know what you mean, I know what you're trying to say . . . Charlie?

Charles Yes?

Bert No sweat, OK? I get it, Charlie. You find it – what's that again? – coarse, right?

Charles Well, yes, yes if you must –

Bert I like it, I like it, Charlie, fucken *coarse*, great word, don't you go worrying about my coarse language, OK?

Charles Um . . .

Bert *lies back.* **Charles** *frowns and heads towards the bathroom.*

Bert Hey, open the window if you're cutting logs in there, OK?

Charles Cutting logs?

Bert Figure o' speech: American. Just open the window, just do me a favour and open the window if you can reach it.

Charles *enters the bathroom,* **Bert** *laughs to himself.*

Bert . . . fucken jerk!

Charles *returns from the bathroom, shoves the chair to where the phone is and climbs up. He picks it up.*

Charles Um, yes, ah, this is Mr Charles Merryweather in room – yes, yes, of course I'll hold . . . (*Turning to* **Bert**.) There's no paper in there.

Bert You really gonna let that fucken harlot on the desk know you need to take a shit? Don't shatter the whore's illusion o' midgets. I got some paper in my case you can borrow, and when I say borrow I ain't meaning I want it back, you get my drift?

Charles *puts the phone down and gets off the chair.* **Bert** *climbs down from the bed, opens his case and hands* **Charles** *a toilet roll (three times the regular size).*

Bert   . . . stayed in these roach hotels before. Last thing they think of in these fucken roach hotels is ass-wipes.

Charles (*heading back to bathroom*)   That's very generous. Thank you.

Bert   Hey, think nothing of it. Us midgets gotta stick together. We're a dying breed, I heard somewhere we're gonna be extinct by the fifties, I don't listen to gossip though.

Charles   That's – where did you hear *that?*

Bert   I told you, kid: I don't listen to gossip, and you know something, you know something and you want my advice, you don't listen to it either, OK?

Charles   . . . Right. Thank you. I won't.

Charles *pauses and closes the door behind him.*

Bert *goes to* **Charles***'s drawer and rummages through it. He finds a wad of dollar bills. He smiles to himself, peels a couple off and looks as though he is about to pocket them. He stops, thinks better of it, puts them back in the wad and closes the drawer. He goes to his case and pulls out a pipe (three times the regular size) and a small package wrapped in brown paper. He fetches the chair and climbs up on the bed. He goes through the ritual of packing the pipe and lighting it up.*

Charles *returns from the bathroom, holding the toilet roll. He looks on as* **Bert** *smokes the pipe.* **Bert** *notices* **Charles***'s shock.*

Bert   Whatsamatter? You never seen a bronchiatric dwarf before? I gotta smoke this shit; opens up the lungs.

Charles   Oh, dear, excuse me, I didn't mean to . . . I didn't mean to stare.

Bert   Kind o' fucken upbringing you ain't ever seen no bronchiatric dwarf, huh?

Charles *puts the toilet roll down next to* **Bert***'s case.* **Bert** *tokes on the pipe and settles back on to the bed.* **Charles** *puts his hands in his*

pockets and paces around, every now and then looking over at **Bert**.
Bert *is now nodding in and out of consciousness.*

Charles   Are you all right, Mr Kowalski?

Long pause.

Bert   Kinda shit did you do back in England, Charlie?

Charles   Sorry?

Bert   Work. What kinda work ya do? There ain't blue
blood in those little veins of yours . . . you ain't like fucken
royalty or shit back there, are ya?

Charles (*bowing his head*)   Oh no . . . no. Nothing like that!
Although I did have a position as a gardener at the Royal
Gardens in Kew.

Bert *picks up the pipe and package.*

Bert   . . . thought I could be in the presence of fucken *royalty*
. . . you just never know nowadays . . . Could you . . . put
these back in my case, Charlie . . . put these back in my
case . . .

Charles *climbs up on to the bed and picks up the pipe as* **Bert** *nods
off.*

We heard thumping and shuffling noises as the door opens. **Raymond**
*– late forties, American, well spoken, well dressed, holding a large case,
stands at the threshold.*

Offstage, we hear the voice again.

Booming male voice (*off*)   In there, little fella, try not to
get up to any mischief.

Charles *cowers in fear of the voice but* **Raymond** *looks up evenly
at its source.*

Raymond   If I were four feet taller I'd take you outside and
give you a damn good thrashing, young man.

Booming male voice (*off*)   Ha, ha, ha. Hey, Harry, we
got a funny dwarf here. Take me outside, ha, ha, ha.

Raymond *puts the case on the bed. Then he pulls in another large leather bag and closes the door. He stares at* **Bert** *and* **Charles**. **Charles** *climbs off the bed with the instruments.*

Raymond   Philistines!

Charles (*offering his hand*)   Charles Merryweather, London, England.

He notices **Raymond** *staring at the pipe. He starts to pack the instruments into* **Bert**'s *case.*

Poor Mr Kowalski suffers from a bronchial complaint.

Raymond *shakes his head and wanders around the room, still holding his case.*

Raymond   And you're his *nurse*, right?

Charles (*heading over to him*)   I see what you mean, no, I'm a Munchkin like you.

Raymond *glares at* **Charles**, *goes over to a bed and throws his bag up on it.*

Raymond   Four beds. Any other 'ailments' I should know about?

Charles (*offering his hand again*)   Charles Merryweather, London, England.

Raymond (*shaking hands*)   Benedict-Porter. Raymond.

Raymond's *grip is strong and Charles winces a little.*

Charles   Pleased to meet you Mr Ben-ah, Mr Por . . . um, which do you prefer?

As they break grip he rubs his hand.

Raymond   Both, but Raymond will suffice.

Charles   Raymond? Excellent . . . Charles or Charlie, I don't have a preference. My friends call me Charles or Charlie. I really don't mind. Whichever you prefer, Mr . . . ah . . . Raymond.

Raymond   Charles sounds more dignified. Yes, I'll call you Charles. Charlie sounds common. There's far too much bastardisation of our language going on, don't you think?

Bert (*asleep, shouting*)   NO!

Charles *and* **Raymond** *stare at* **Bert**. **Raymond** *shakes his head and goes to the chest of drawers and unpacks his case.* **Charles** *stands with him.*

Charles   Jolly good storyplay.

Raymond   I prefer the book.

Charles   You prefer the *book*?

Raymond   The storyplay has been adapted from a book. You didn't know that?

Charles   A book, no.

Raymond   Yes.

Charles   Which book? From which book has it been . . . ah . . .

Raymond (*sighing*)   *The Wonderful Wizard of Oz.*

Charles   Oh.

Raymond   Yes. Very popular.

Charles   I see, I see, they've simply abandoned the 'wonderful'?

Raymond   Quite . . . Is this your first 'acting' role?

Charles   Yes, well, no, I mean, I had a small part in an amateur production of *A Midsummer's Night Dream* in Deptford. It got cancelled after the second night and I think it was a *very* amateur production.

Raymond   Amateur?

Charles   I think so. Nobody was paid.

Raymond   I toured extensively with *Richard III*.

Charles   Really?

Raymond   Mmm, extensively.

Charles   Whom did you – did you play?

Raymond   Richard of course.

Charles   Richard, right . . . Wasn't he a hunchback?

Raymond *closes the drawer and heads off towards the bathroom.*

Raymond   Not *just* a hunchback, not simply a hunchback.

Charles   I'm not familiar, but I recall him being a hunchback.

Raymond   Quite, he was, but he was much more besides. He was much more than a hunchback.

Charles   There's no paper in there, Mr Benedict-Porter.

Raymond   No paper?

Charles   No, no paper, Mr Kowal—

Raymond   Why do you assume I need to evacuate my bowels? Do I look like I'm in need of a bowel *movement*?

Charles   No, no, I just –

Raymond   Not that I'm not regular, you understand, on the contrary. Nothing wrong with my bowel movements: like clockwork. Are you a sufferer?

Charles   *Sufferer*?

Raymond   Constipation . . . do you get 'bunged up', dear boy?

Charles   Um.

Raymond   Just say if you do, nothing to be *ashamed* of, just speak out if you do because I've a cure for constipation if you're a sufferer. Very simple cure, just say if you're –

Charles   No, no, no, I'm – I'm not a sufferer. I don't – no, not constipation. I've a friend though, a friend who's a . . . I suppose you could call him a sufferer.

Raymond   I can't help him: your friend. It's a hands-on cure, very simple. It involves freeing up the colonic passage. Takes no time at all. Very common among small people. Yes, a common complaint I suppose you could call it, but I'm afraid I can't help your friend though, hands on, you understand? I take it your friend's back in England?

Charles   Yes, yes he's still there. I think he's still in England.

Raymond   London?

Charles   Yes . . .

Raymond   Does he know of Frederick Matthias Alexander? He runs a school there. An Australian originally. An actor by training. I'm a great disciple of his technique; it has such widespread application.

Charles   I don't know any Australians in London . . . and I'm sure my friend wouldn't either.

Raymond   As I thought, shame really, a real shame, very simple and effective. Takes no time at all. It can be very painful, I hear?

Charles   It can?

Raymond   *Constipation.*

Charles   I, ah, I really wouldn't know.

Raymond   No . . . no, neither would I, but I've heard it can be horrendously painful.

Charles   I suppose, I mean, I'd imagine it would be.

Raymond   So I'm told . . . so people have *said.*

Suddenly **Bert** *groans.* **Charles** *and* **Raymond** *look over at him.* **Raymond** *goes into the bathroom.*

Charles *goes and takes a close look at* **Bert**. *After a while he picks up the script from the floor and paces around reading it aloud.*

Charles (*poorly reading the Cowardly Lion's lines out loud*)   'Put 'em up . . . This is great . . . 'rhinoceros, imposserus' . . .

He laughs as he marvels at the script.

Raymond (*entering with two glasses and going to his case*)   Would you care for a libation? I hate to drink alone. I find it leaves a sour taste . . .

Charles *watches* **Raymond** *pull out a bottle of Scotch (three times the regular size) from his case.*

Charles   Ah, I don't usually – not really my cup of tea, whisky, I'm not really a whisky –

Raymond (*pouring the drinks*)   Nonsense, there you go.

Charles *reluctantly takes the glass and sips from it as* **Raymond** *downs his in one and pours himself another.* **Bert** *grunts again.* **Raymond** *looks across at him.*

Raymond   We should maybe turn him on his side. An acquaintance of mine choked on vomit.

Charles   Oh dear.

Raymond   Nasty business.

Charles   His own, was it? The vomit that he choked on?

Raymond   His *own*?

Charles   Vomit.

Raymond (*frowning*)   He didn't strike me as the kind of person who would ingest other people's vomit. And yes he did survive and thank you for your concern. I'll give you a hand.

They climb up on to **Bert***'s bed and turn him on his side. They climb back down.*

You're not going to join me?

Charles (*handing the full glass back to him*)   Um, no. I was
made to – I tried it once. It didn't agree with me. I got
terrible heartburn.

Raymond   Heartburn?

Charles   Terrible heartburn.

Raymond   Afraid I can't help you there. Constipation:
different kettle of fish. Now if it were constipation you were
talking about . . . No, heartburn's not my specialty.

He takes the bottle of whisky over to the chair, climbs up and sits down.
Charles *pulls up a chair next to him.*

So, tell me, what're you doing out here?

Charles   Out here?

Raymond   In Culver City in the year of Our Lord
nineteen hundred and thirty-five, yes.

Charles   Ah, I'm going to be a Munchkin, I'm going to be
a Munchkin just like you and Mr Kowalski, Mr Porter.

Raymond   Quite . . . but how did you find out about the
production? I can see you're not a real actor and do please
call me Raymond, Charles.

Charles   I will, thank you, Raymond.

Raymond   Think nothing of it.

Charles   You're most kind.

Raymond   Quite. Now, as I was saying, I can see you're
not an actor.

Charles   Oh, does it . . . ah, does it *show*?

Raymond (*scrutinising* **Charles**)   It's not *obvious*, but then
one needs a trained actor's eye to spot a fellow thesp.

Charles   A *trained* eye?

Raymond   To spot a fellow thespian.

Charles   So . . . so I'm *obviously not* an actor in your eye?

Raymond   Quite.

Charles   I didn't . . . there didn't seem to be a problem. They asked for – I sent them a photograph and they –

Raymond   No, no, no, forget – just forget about photographs. You're confusing the map with the terrain. Of course they wouldn't be able to determine whether you're a *real* actor from a photograph.

Charles   Right. I see, but –

Raymond   How did you hear about the production?

Charles   Well, a friend of a friend told me –

Raymond   The sufferer?

Charles   Sufferer?

Raymond   The constipated friend, the sufferer. He's the friend of a friend?

Charles   Oh, no, I see, no, no, he's just a friend. It was another friend, well, a friend of a friend, he, he told me they were looking for . . . for people like me. I've always wanted to come and visit the United States, I've never seen a palm tree or a Californian redwood, and I thought –

Raymond   Yip Harburg and Harold Arlen insisted that I come on board.

Charles   Oh, ah –

Raymond   The composers: Harburg and Arlen. Yip and Harold.

Charles   Oh, right . . . um, so when I heard –

Raymond   Close friends of mine . . . they've written an adorable song called 'Over the Rainbow', unfortunately the studio don't feel that it fits in with the tone of the rest of the compositions. Terrible waste. Very close friends.

Charles   Oh, yes, I can imagine . . . Anyway this friend of a friend –

Raymond   I wonder who's going to be joining us. I do hope it's a fellow thesp.

Charles   I, ah, I wouldn't know, but as I was saying –

Raymond   You're not one of the Washington Merryweathers by any chance? You're not related?

Charles   Washington Merryweathers, um, I don't –

Raymond   Lovely people. Lionel's a hoot. We were in the Scottish play together.

Charles   *Macbeth?*

Raymond   Ah, you see . . . if I hadn't already worked out you're not a thesp I'd have known you weren't by now.

Charles   Oh . . . I see. So you weren't recruited by Mr Singer, the circus impresario? Mr Kowalski says that the studio gave him the contract to recruit all the Munchkins.

Raymond   I don't know anything about a Mr Singer. (*Standing up and wandering over to look at* **Bert**.) What is it you expect to find out here?

Charles   Find? What do you mean *find*?

Raymond   I mean find in the sense of . . . the everyday common sensical definition.

Charles   Right.

Raymond   You see, everyone – and by that I mean absolutely everyone – *everyone* who comes out here hopes to find *something*. That 'something' usually being the pot of gold.

Charles   Aaaahhhh, I understand.

Raymond   So?

Charles   Am I out here for the –

Raymond   I don't know. Are you? People usually are, that's what they're usually out here looking for.

Charles   Well, I *would* like to see some of the exotic plants and flowers that grow in warmer climates. Flora and fauna have always fascinated me so if I think about it, I suppose I am, I am out here looking for *something*.

Raymond   Never mind flowers and *something*, what're you doing out here, what's the real motivation?

Charles *frowns and pauses.*

Charles   Well, ah, as I was saying, this friend of a friend told me that they were looking for people like me out here and I –

Raymond   Don't let me interrupt you.

Charles   Oh, ah, right, so anyway, anyway this –

Raymond   Don't take it personally. I don't even know you. For all I know you may very well be an intelligent young man.

Charles   No, no, of course not. So as I was –

Raymond   I'm not judgemental.

Charles   No, no, I don't think for one moment –

Raymond   Can't afford to be, Charles. Not in my profession: kiss of death. I'm an empty vessel, you see. We need to be tuned into all walks of life, keep in step as I say . . . No, no, no, no, no I'm not judgemental. Don't take it personally. Don't be offended.

Charles   No, I really . . . I really understand what you're saying, Raymond.

Raymond   Actors are empty vessels waiting to be – oh listen to me going on . . .

A long pause. **Raymond** *goes into his suitcase and takes out a sleeveless top. He unbuttons his shirt, carefully taking off two outsized* *gold cufflinks, which he carefully puts on the top of his locker. Then he strips to the waist and puts on his sleeveless top. His muscles bulge. He goes into the leather bag and pulls out two outsized barbells.*

Charles   Anyway . . .

Raymond *starts doing arm curls with the barbells.*

Raymond   Kowalski. You say he's called Kowalski?

Charles   Yes . . . um, Bert.

Raymond   Oh, please don't mind me. I like to keep in tip-top physical condition. Do you exercise?

Charles   No, but I did do gardening work in London. Outdoors . . . very healthy work.

Raymond (*looking him over*)   Hmm . . . all good and well, but you should attempt to keep up a satisfactory level of fitness. A film set can be a demanding environment, physically and mentally. Healthy body, healthy mind. (*Looks across at* **Bert**.) So it's Bert, eh . . . Bert Kowalski?

Charles   That's right. Bert Kowalski. Do you know him?

Raymond   No, Bert Kowalski doesn't ring any bells. Might not be his real name though. Did he claim to be an actor?

Charles   Um, I don't think so . . . he does use very coarse language though.

Raymond   He does? Really? How coarse? How coarse are we talking?

Charles   Oh it's very –

Raymond   Profanities?

Charles   Pro—

Raymond   He's profane?

Charles   Ah, I wouldn't know, I can't really say, but he uses very coarse words. Very *vulgar* for a short man with a bronchial complaint. I think we got off on the wrong –

Raymond *puts down the barbells. He gets his breath then starts another routine.*

Raymond   Very coarse language, eh? Could be a thesp, could well be a thesp.

Charles   An actor?

Raymond   Could be, wouldn't be *unheard* of if he were.

Charles   I don't know, but it could be his, you know, it could be his condition. His bronchitis, I'm only assuming but . . . well, I mean you never know, do you?

Raymond   If he is indeed *profane* there could well be a reason behind it.

Charles   Yes?

Raymond   Oh yes. Oh yes indeed, but we'd only be guessing and guessing games invariably lead to confusion. My experience . . .

Raymond *drops the weights and rolls them under his bed.*

Charles   Yes?

Raymond   Yes, it can lead to confusion.

Pause.

Charles   Probably best not guessing then –

Raymond   Quite.

Charles   You're right. I probably shouldn't guess.

Raymond   Wise, wise of you because it makes sense, in the long run in my experience, it makes sense. You're a very wise . . . (*Pause as he looks* **Bert** *over.*) *Cunt.*

Charles   I beg your –

Raymond   Did he use the C word? Very emotive word, cunt . . . a lot of thesps use it. Lionel Merryweather can be relied upon to pepper any conversation with a cunt or two . . . very emotive word. It's in the dictionary, you know?

Charles   Oh . . . ah –

Raymond   You didn't *know*?

Charles   . . . mmm . . .

Raymond   It's of Teutonic origin of course. Very emotive.
I'm an admirer of emotive words. Being an actor, you
understand . . . my tools: emotive words. Being an actor you
need sharp precise tools. *Cunt* is a great *tool*. I'm more fond of
it than, I don't know, say for instance 'fuck' off the top of my
head . . . fuck is losing its resonance if you want my opinion.
Far too common a curse: fuck. Very rare you hear hoi polloi
employing cunts in their limited vocabularies. At least here. I
wouldn't know about England.

Charles   Oh, ah, well, my mother always says –

Raymond   Abuse, you see, common everyday abuse, it's
rendered fuck impotent. It's everywhere nowadays. Let's just
hope cunt doesn't become as commonplace. One of the few
emotive taboo words we have left to play with: cunt.

Charles   Right.

Raymond   It's got a very precise sound to it. Cunt's a
precision tool.

Raymond *pours himself another large whisky. He offers the bottle to*
Charles. **Charles** *shakes his head, he tries to hide his
embarrassment by picking up the script.*

Charles   Fascinating read.

Raymond   Noel's done a fantastic job.

Charles   Noel?

Raymond   Noel Langley, the scenarist. I'm going to be
playing the Mayor by the way.

Charles   The Mayor?

Charles *scours the script.* **Raymond** *sighs heavily and points*
Charles *to the right page.*

Raymond   The Mayor of the . . . there, look.

Charles   Oh, yes, silly me, the Mayor of the Munchkins. That's really, I mean it sounds so . . . well, it sounds really *grand*. Mayor of Munchkinland. You must be really pleased. I don't, what do you think . . . ? Probably just have me in the background, I suppose. Probably something really small. Not like you though, eh: Mayor of Munchkinland. You must be very proud of yourself.

Bert *groans and turns over.* **Raymond** *and* **Charles** *look over at him.* **Bert** *lets out a loud fart, smiles to himself and turns back over.* **Raymond** *carries on as usual.*

Raymond   So you're going to be an extra then?

Charles   An extra?

Raymond   An extra Mu— an extra small person.

Charles   I couldn't rightly say. A man from the studio picked me up at the station, he picked me up, brought me here and told me to stay put until I heard otherwise. I suppose it will be, I mean it's bound to be something small. A small part, I should imagine.

Raymond   Yes, you're bound to be an *extra* small person. I'm surprised I'm having to share with an extra though. I must make a mental note to bring it up with Mr LeRoy.

Charles   Mervyn! I mean, Mr LeRoy! You know Mr – you're going to bring it up with Mr Mervyn LeRoy? You *know* him?

Raymond   Intimately. We've worked together.

Charles   Really? You've worked with Mr LeRoy?

Raymond   We go back a long way.

Charles   You go back with Mr Mervin LeRoy, well I never. Who'd have thought I'd be sharing a room with . . . well, I mean, that's just –

Raymond   Must be an oversight.

Charles   Oversight?

Raymond   Sharing: having to *share*.

Charles   Right, I see.

Raymond   A little word in Mervyn's ear should remedy it.

Charles   It must be – I mean, you're not used to sharing with extra small people.

Raymond   No, don't take it personally, don't take it as a personal attack, you understand.

Charles   No, of course –

Raymond   I've nothing against you, Charles. You know that, don't you?

Charles   Yes.

Raymond   Yes, of course you do. I hardly know you, we've hardly got to know each other.

Charles   Of course.

Raymond   I feel I can trust you though, Charles. Something tells me I can trust you.

Charles   Yes?

Raymond   Oh yes, I'm intuitive. If there's one thing I am it's intuitive.

Charles   I'm glad you feel you can –

Raymond   There's no doubt.

Charles   Well, I'm flattered.

Raymond   My credo . . . (*Pause.*) . . . Well?

Charles   Sorry?

Raymond   My credo: ask me what it is?

Charles   Mmm: what is your . . . ah . . . ?

Raymond   Credo?

Charles   Yes.

Raymond   My credo is trust, Charles.

Charles   Oh, right, I see, I see.

Raymond   Nothing means more to me than trust.

Charles   Really?

Raymond   No . . . no, if I can't have trust I can't have *anything*.

Charles   That's very . . . ah . . .

Raymond   Quite. So now you know and your mind should be set firmly at rest around me. I am a man of *trust* and I *know* you are too, Charles.

Charles   Thank you . . . Raymond.

Raymond   Think nothing of it.

Charles   No, no, it's really, It's really ah, really thoughtful of you.

Raymond   What are we *without* thoughts?

Charles   That's true.

Raymond   Nothing.

Charles   Yes.

Raymond   Without thoughts we are nothing.

Charles   I know.

Raymond   True, and trust comes out of truth.

Charles   It does?

Raymond   You don't think so?

Charles   Um, I haven't really –

Raymond   It does, Charles: trust me.

Charles   I will, I will.

Raymond   Good.

Charles   I'm glad you can trust me, Raymond. It makes me feel really . . . really at home.

Raymond (*tapping his nose and winking*)   Buddy Ebsen's in an iron lung and that's from the horse's mouth.

Charles   . . . 'Buddy Ebsen's in an iron lung and that's –' . . . can't say I've heard of it. Is it a moving picture or a theatre play?

Raymond   No, no, Buddy Ebsen was cast as the Tin Woodsman. He kept inhaling aluminum dust and they've had to put him in an iron lung for his own protection.

Charles   What sort of dust is that?

Raymond   Aluminum dust . . . you must have aluminum in England?

Charles   Al-u-min-ium?

Raymond   Al-u-what? *Aluminum*, dear chap. There's enough bastardisation of our language without you English . . .

He realises what he's saying and pauses.

Charles   Oh . . . dear, that's . . . that's just – an iron lung? Dear me.

Raymond (*conspiratorially*)   Keep it to yourself but Jack Haley's going to be taking his place. Jack's going to be the Tin Woodsman but that's strictly between you and me, it's not become official yet, but feel free to quote your source when it becomes so.

Charles *ponders this for a while, scratching his head and turning to* **Raymond**.

Charles   But . . .

Raymond   Yes?

Charles   Well, I mean . . . why would he want to do such a thing?

Raymond   A *thing*?

Charles   A thing, yes.

Raymond   Dear boy, an actor's life is precarious at the best of times. Jack Haley can't be frowned upon for stepping into Buddy Ebsen's Tin Woodsman shoes.

Charles   No, no, no. The man? The man in the iron lung? Why would he *want* to inhale aluminium . . . huh, *aluminum* dust? Why would the man in the iron lung want to inhale the dust in the first place?

Raymond *sighs heavily, finishes off his whisky and pours another large one.*

Raymond   He didn't want to inhale aluminum – *al-u-min-ium* dust in the first place.

Charles   No?

Raymond   No, definitely not. He most certainly didn't want to inhale the dust.

Charles   I see . . . he was *compelled*?

Raymond   He was inhaling the dust from the make-up they were applying to him so as to make him look metallic.

Charles   Aaahhh, right, I see. He was inhaling, huh, aluminum dust *accidentally*.

Raymond   That's right, there was nothing compelling about the inhalation.

Charles   No?

Raymond   Absolutely not.

Charles   What bad luck.

Raymond   Bad luck? Bad luck doesn't even enter into it, Charles. Luck is not the issue here.

Charles   It isn't?

Bert *wakes up and watches them. They are unaware of him.*

Raymond   No. Negligence is – I believe – the word that sums up this sorry state of affairs.

Charles   Right. I understand.

Raymond   I know you do, Charles. I know you understand because you are a very understanding young man.

Charles   Yes? You think so?

Raymond   There is no need to be bashful, Charles.

Charles   Oh, huh, I didn't realise I was being –

Raymond   It's unbecoming.

Charles   Oh, right . . . I see.

Raymond   Trust and understanding go hand in hand, Charles.

Bert   Any of that malt looking for a home?

Charles *and* **Raymond** *turn and look at* **Bert** *in surprise.*

Charles (*going over to* **Bert**)   Ah, Mr Kowalski, this is Mr . . . ah –

Raymond (*pouring a glass for* **Bert**)   Benedict-Porter. Raymond Benedict-Por—

Bert   I know who he is, Charlie, I know who he is. Used to be the most in-demand midget on the circuit . . .

Raymond *hands up the glass of whisky to* **Bert**. **Bert** *knocks it back in one and holds the glass back out to* **Raymond**.

Bert   . . . man's a legend in littledom.

Charles *is impressed.* **Raymond** *pours* **Bert** *another shot and smiles to himself as* **Bert** *climbs down off the bed and takes the glass from him.*

Raymond   I wouldn't go as far as to say *legend*.

Bert *climbs up on to a chair and smiles at* **Raymond**.

Bert   No, guess you wouldn't. Guess you wouldn't call yourself a legend. You're too modest, right?

A pause as **Raymond** *and* **Bert** *eye each other.* **Raymond** *pulls off his top and puts his shirt back on.* **Charles** *breaks the ice.*

Charles   We're all going to be Munchkins. We're all going to be Munchkins together.

Bert   That's right, Charlie, we're all going down that yellow brick road.

Charles   I can't wait.

Raymond   Actually the Mu— it's only Dorothy and her friends who get to travel down the yellow brick road.

Bert   Wichita.

Raymond   . . . Wichita?

Bert   'Twenty-nine. We worked the circus, remember?

A long pause as **Raymond** *tries to remember.*

Raymond   . . . No, no, you've lost me there, Mr Kowalski. Can't recall ever performing in Wichita.

Bert   Fred Corelli's troupe, you must remember. We were the flying fucken dwarfs f'chrissakes.

Raymond   Flying . . . no, no, I can't . . .

He downs his whisky and pours himself another shot, finishing off the bottle.

Oh dear, the well's run dry.

He goes to his case and pulls out another bottle.

Bert   Guess it was a long time ago: 'twenty-nine. Guess 'twenty-nine was years ago.

Raymond (*opening the bottle and approaching* **Bert**)   I'm sure I'd remember 'twenty-nine.

Bert   Yeah, I'm sure you would. How can you forget the flying fucken dwarfs?

Raymond   I'd have remembered.

Bert   Yeah, you would remember. Anyone'd remember flying, right?

Raymond *pours himself and* **Bert** *another glass.*

Charles   Um, anyone know what time dinner's served? I could eat a horse.

Bert   Yeah, but could you eat a horse of a different colour, Charlie?

Charles   A different colour? A horse of –

Raymond   Mr Kowalski's referring to the horse of a different colour from the storyplay, Charles. He is being *witty*.

Charles   Right.

Bert   Jerking you off, Charlie.

Raymond   *Pulling your leg* I believe is the vernacular, Charles.

Charles   Oh, no, no, it was merely a figure of speech, I didn't mean –

Bert   Yeah, I know. I know what you mean, Charlie. I know you ain't figuring on eating a horse of a different colour. Any horse-eating gonna be done in here n' I wanna know about it. I know you ain't a horse eater, Charlie.

Bert *drains his glass and holds it out.*

Raymond   Dinner's served at seven, Charles. In answer to your question, that is.

Charles   It is?

Raymond   Yes: seven.

Charles (*checking his outsized watch*)   Seven? Splendid.

Raymond   I wouldn't get too excited. The cuisine here is dreadful. There's a wonderful little restaurant across the street, we should eat there.

Charles   Oh . . . I was, ah, I was planning to have all my meals here. I'm a little, I haven't really –

Bert   Whatever ya do, don't go to that crummy joint. Met one little guy at the desk when I booked in, he'd gotten here yesterday – Tiny Taylor – he told me to pass on that joint. Said he didn't know what they put in the food but it sat like a fucken rock in his gut all night.

Charles *is now looking really uncomfortable, a fact not lost on* **Raymond**.

Raymond   Everything all right?

Bert   Maybe Charlie's on a tight budget. Tight budgets all the rage round here. Maybe Charlie wants to be all the rage. Tight fucken budgets! Makes you wanna turn to drink, uh, Ray?

Raymond *gets* **Bert**'*s hint and tops up the glasses.* **Bert** *looks over at the fourth bed and finishes off his whisky.*

Bert   Wonder where the missing Munchkin is.

Charles   So was I. I was wondering.

Raymond   *Assuming* it is a small person.

Pause.

Charles   Oh . . . you don't, you don't think they'd put a *big* person in here with us, do you, Raymond?

Raymond   A big *person*?

Charles   Yes, you know, a, a –

Bert   A regular guy. You mean a regular guy, right, Charlie?

Raymond   Does that worry you, Charles?

Bert   Does it, Charlie? It worries you?

Charles   Well, ah, I don't, I mean. It would make more sense to keep us all together, wouldn't it? I just thought we'd all be Munchkins in here together.

Raymond   No no no, there's definitely a note of anxiety in your voice. You're worried, aren't you?

Charles   I'm not *worried*, I just feel, I've nothing against big people, I know lots of big people and I'm not worried. I just, well, I suppose it makes sense. I suppose, what I, what I'm trying to –

Bert   Don't sweat it, Charlie. This is Munchkin central. There's gonna be no integration. Two hundred midgets under the same roof. They gotta be able to keep an eye on us. Can't have midgets running riot around Culver City. Bad for publicity.

Charles   Yes, yes you're right, it makes sense . . .

Raymond   I can't imagine what on earth you'd have to *fear* from big people, Charles. Some of the kindest people I've ever met have been of regular stature.

Bert   Biggest heels I met been big people. Condescending cocksuckers. This gig ain't gonna be any different . . .

Charles   . . . they'll always know where the Munchkins *are*.

Bert   . . . beats the fucken soup kitchen though. Just about beats the soup kitchen and there's very little in it you wanna know the truth.

Raymond   I wouldn't know.

Charles   If we're all under the same roof it makes sense.

Raymond   I have to disagree with you, Mr Kowalski: soup kitchens? Please! I believe this picture will be a resounding success. Mr LeRoy is a genius, and it's common knowledge that Mr Louis B. Mayer himself is right behind the enterprise. One hundred per cent behind it, I heard.

Bert   That right, is it? The gospel?

Raymond   From upon high: good sources.

Charles (*to himself*)   We'd get under their feet.

Bert   You in for a cut of the profits, Ray?

Raymond   *Money* isn't the point.

Bert   Nothing wrong with dough.

Raymond   I'm not saying there is.

Bert   Don't knock dough, Ray.

Raymond   *Raymond.*

Bert   You knock dough, we ain't pissing on the same patch. You got some knockout broad on Hollywood Boulevard, legs so fucken long you gotta stand on Charlie's shoulders to get a sniff o' her sweet pie; she ain't gonna look twice at the likes of us. But you got a big bunch o' greenbacks in your tail, you ain't no short-assed gnome no more.

Raymond   I'd hardly –

Bert   What, Ray? Leave money out o' this: you got a beef with money you need examining.

Raymond   Please, Mr Kowalski; I have a point that needs getting across.

Bert   Point away, Ray.

Pause.

Raymond   The *point* here isn't the money. I'm proud to be associated with a moving picture of such high production values. I really believe it has quality. It's a timeless story. Don't you agree, Charles?

Charles   Agree with what?

Raymond   That it's a timeless story. *The Wonderful Wizard of Oz*?

Charles   Um, yes, ah . . . I love the Cowardly Lion . . .

He grabs a hold of the script and flips the pages. **Bert** *shakes his head and pours himself another whisky.*

Charles (*reading the lines*)   'Put 'em up' . . . very funny. That's just . . . well, I mean, it's very, very funny. I think it'll be very funny when it's finished. Your friend is a very funny writer. (*Pause.*) So you don't, you really don't think they'll be putting big people in here with us?

Raymond   What attracts me is the universal theme of finding happiness in your own backyard, so to speak.

Bert   Where is your backyard nowadays, Ray?

Raymond   Washington and it's Raymond if you don't mind.

Bert   So you got out o' Detroit, uh?

Raymond   Detroit? I –

Bert   I told you. We worked out in Wichita together, 'twenty-nine, Fred Corelli's troupe, flying fucken dwarfs. How could you forget the flying fucken dwarfs, Ray? You were the catcher, you had to catch me in those strong mitts of yours.

Raymond   . . . 'Twenty-nine, you say?

Charles   I can't see them putting big people in here really.

Bert   That's right: 'twenty-nine. Flying fucken dwarfs.

Raymond *ponders, pulls out his cigarette case and offers one to* **Charles** *and* **Bert**. *They all light up.*

Raymond   . . . Wichita . . . um . . .

Charles   Is that prairie country?

Bert   Uh?

Charles   Wichita, Kansas. Grasslands. I'd imagine there'd be nothing interesting or exotic regarding flora and fauna. Am I right?

Raymond   I really can't recall working in Wichita in 'twenty-nine . . . no, you've lost me in Wichita, I'm afraid.

Bert   You should maybe ask the marvellous Mr LeRoy if he can arrange a meeting with the Wonderful Wizard . . . you could ask him to fix you up a memory, Ray.

Charles   Wichita. Is there a lot of agriculture around Wichita, Bert? Cattle country, I'm assuming.

Raymond   It's impossible for one to keep track of all one's appearances, Mr Kowalski. I'm sure you'd understand if you were as in demand.

Bert   I'm sure I would.

Raymond   Yes.

Bert   Sure.

Charles   I've always wanted to see a Californian redwood. There are trees so big that they've been hollowed out so that motor cars can drive through them. I would doubt that Wichita is a heavily forested area though, eh, Bert?

Bert   Maybe not so many trees in Wichita, Charlie, but there's a hell of a lot o' skeletons rattling in closets.

Bert *glares at* **Raymond**. **Raymond** *wanders about the room. A large envelope is slid under the door. Nobody notices.*

Raymond   . . . I promise you'll be the first to know if my memory recalls anything pertaining to Wichita in 'twenty-nine, Mr Kowalski.

Suddenly **Charles** *catches sight of the large envelope. He goes over and picks it up.*

Charles   . . . It's addressed to Kowalski, Merryweather, Benedict-Porter and Kinsella. I think Kinsella might well be our missing Munchkin.

Raymond   Obviously.

Raymond *takes the envelope out of* **Charles***'s hand and starts to open it.*

Bert   Don't you think we should maybe wait for Kinsella, Ray?

Raymond   Kinsella might never show up.

Bert   You don't think?

Raymond   It could happen.

Bert   That Kinsella *won't* show?

Raymond   No. Kinsella might show. There's also a possibility that Kinsella won't show.

Bert   You know *these* things, uh?

Raymond   Look –

Bert   Go ahead, you were saying, Ray.

Raymond   I *was*, I was saying it could be important – this letter – and for the umpteenth time it's Raymond *and/*or Benedict-Porter.

Bert   If it were important the desk would o' called. It ain't professional opening other midgets' mail. Besides, Kinsella might be one of those touchy midgets that get real pissed if they think they're getting left out. You know the sort, Ray.

Raymond   I don't know 'the sort'.

Bert   Sure you do: uppity fucken midgets.

Raymond   I really can't see what harm it would do.

Charles   I think Raymond's right, Bert. I'm sure Mr Kinsella would realise we're only –

Bert   You *know* Kinsella, Charlie?

Charles   No, we've never, obviously not . . . but –

Bert   For all you, me, Ray there, all we know Kinsella's a
real cranky evil little sonofabitch. Think about it, Charlie,
you're gonna be sharing a room with him for weeks, you
don't wanna be making enemies with dwarfs you don't even
know yet.

Raymond   I'll take full responsibility if Mr Kinsella finds
the gesture untoward.

Bert   *Untoward*?

Raymond   That's what I said.

Bert   I heard you: you're saying *untoward*.

Raymond   Correct.

Bert   OK.

Raymond   There's no harm.

Charles   Can I just –

Bert   No harm, uh? Nothing *untoward*, right?

Charles   Please, Mr –

Bert   Call me Bert.

Charles   Mr Kowalski, I'm trying to . . . look . . .

Raymond *starts to open the envelope again.* **Charles** *moves over to*
Raymond.

Charles   Um, maybe Mr Kowalski's right about –

Raymond   Charles, this is between me and the missing Mr
Kinsella. Who, if we're being realistic, might never show . . .
there are more unprofessional small people out there than
you could ever dream of.

Bert   You don't even know he's an unprofessional midget,
Ray. Anything could o' happened to the little guy. Culver's a
big city. He could o' got lost. Even giants get lost in
Hollywood, Ray.

Charles   Bert *has* got a point, Raymond.

Raymond   You're an authority on who gets lost and who doesn't get lost in Hollywood now, Charles?

Charles   I, huh –

Bert   Kid's got a point.

Raymond   You're an aficionado now, Charles?

Charles   I wasn't trying to –

Raymond   Then don't.

Bert   Kid's just cautious, Ray.

Raymond   Raymond and/or Benedict-Porter for the last time, Kowalski!

Bert   Kid's entitled to be cautious. Ain't nothing *untoward* going on, eh, uh, Charlie?

Raymond   I've said I'll take full responsibility.

Raymond *pulls out a sheet of paper from the envelope and reads it. His expression slowly turns to one of shock, then anger and finally rage.*

Charles   . . . What is it, Raymond?

Raymond *shoves the paper into* **Charles**'s *hand and storms over to the chair, puts it near the telephone and climbs up.* **Bert** *takes the sheet of paper from* **Charles**, *reads it and laughs out loud.* **Charles** *stands over* **Bert**'s *shoulder.*

Charles   . . . Oh dear, he thought he was going to be the Mayor of Munchkinland.

Bert   Looks like he's gonna have to settle on being third Munchkin soldier from the left . . . plays his cards right, they might elect him one day!

Raymond (*into phone*)   . . . Desk? . . . put me through to Mr LeRoy, this is Mr Raymond Benedict-Porter. (*Long pause.*) . . . Oh, I see . . . (*Furtively putting his hand over the mouthpiece.*) . . . Yes of course, of course I'll hold.

Charles   . . . Mr Kinsella's going to be one of the Lullaby League.

Bert   . . . Had my heart set on being the Coroner.

Charles   I suppose being a Munchkin baby isn't too bad, considering.

Bert   Maybe you get to suck on some Munchkin titties.

Charles   Oh dear. You don't think –

Bert   Ray'd give his high teeth to be a Munchkin baby right now, Charlie.

Raymond (*shoots a disgusted pout at* **Bert** *then speaks into phone*) Ah, Mr LeRoy . . . Mervyn . . . Raymond Benedict-Porter . . . Fine, fine, and you? . . . Oh, good, good . . . Oh yes, yes, and it was a pleasure working with you, Mervyn . . . I hate to bother you . . .

Charles – *frowning* – *and* **Bert** – *shaking his head* – *watch* **Raymond**'s *performance on the telephone.*

Raymond   . . . but ah, I've just received my call sheet . . . That's right, ah, there seems to be a little mistake, well, more of an oversight . . . Do you happen to have your call sheets handy perchance?

Charles   How come he gets to call out and we don't?

Raymond (*into phone*)   . . . Oh, right, I see, I see . . . yes, I thought it must be a mistake . . . yes, I understand. No, no problem . . . Oh yes I'd love to, yes, give us chance to catch up on old times, yes, Mervyn . . . *au revoir.* My regards to Mrs LeRoy . . . Yes, bye.

Raymond *climbs down off the chair and finishes off his whisky.*

Bert   A mistake, uh?

Raymond   Mervyn's given me his assurance it'll be remedied.

Charles   Um, I hate to ask, and I hope you don't feel I'm preying on your good nature, Raymond –

Raymond   These things happen on such large productions, Mr Kowalski . . . but of course you wouldn't know that, would you?

Bert   No, guess I wouldn't. I guess I wouldn't know what happens round these parts.

Charles   Ah, Raymond, I was wondering –

Raymond   Quite.

Bert   Guess we're not all big shots in the world o' entertainment.

Raymond   No.

Bert   Guess I know more about what goes on in places like Wichita, uh?

Charles   I was wondering, Raymond –

Raymond   You're still *performing* in the circus, Mr Kowalski?

Bert   You want me to put in a word someplace?

Raymond (*feigning a chuckle*)   Oh, no, no, I've moved on from circus. I haven't had to lower myself since –

Bert   Wichita, 'twenty-nine?

Charles   Raymond –

Raymond   I was going to say I haven't had to lower myself to circus since –

Bert   Wichita, 'twenty-nine?

Raymond *glares at* **Bert** *and shakes his head.*

Charles   . . . I was wondering if you could make a call out for me, Raymond? I'd be willing to recompense you of course, it's just that I'd like to let my parents know that I've arrived safely. They won't let us make outside calls, you see.

Raymond *is flustered.* **Bert** *stares at* **Raymond**. **Raymond** *bows his head and runs his fingers through his hair.*

Raymond   . . . Ah . . . um . . .

Bert   Well, Ray?

Charles   If it's the money you're –

Raymond   No, no, it's not that, Charles, it's just that I'd feel a little, I mean I've got a relationship with the producers and I'd hate to –

Bert   Cut the crap, Ray, you can't get an outside line. You couldn't get an outside line if this hotel was on fire and all the midgets in here were frying.

Raymond   Don't talk – who do you think I was just talking to?

Bert   Yourself.

Raymond   You think I was –

Bert   Sure.

Raymond   Talking to *myself*?

Bert   We heard ya, Ray.

Raymond   Don't be – why would I want to do that? Why would I want to talk to myself?

Bert   A number of reasons, the chief one being maybe people don't wanna listen to your crap any more.

Raymond *sighs and pours himself a whisky.*

Raymond   Is there something eating you, Mr Kowalski? Something's eating, you seem intent on trying to needle me, *is* something eating you?

Bert   *Eating me?*

Raymond   Yes, something eat— you're trying to needle me.

Bert   Why would I want to needle you, Ray? I don't even know you, remember?

Bert *picks up the toilet roll and goes into the bathroom.* **Charles** *stares at* **Raymond**, *puzzled.*

Charles   . . . You were . . . I mean, on the tele . . . you weren't –

Raymond   Take no notice of the drug fiend. I'll be having words with Mervyn, see if we can't get him off the production.

Charles   I must say, Raymond, I mean, the poor chap's chronically bronchial –

Raymond   Don't be – are you –

Charles   He's coarse but, I mean, his condition is –

Raymond (*laughing*)   Wake up, you idiot! He's an opium addict. If anything has damaged his lungs, it's *smoking opium*.

A long pause. **Charles** *lets* **Raymond**'s *words sink in.*

Charles   . . . Opium? I didn't –

Raymond   Of course you didn't.

Pause.

Charles   You mean . . . ? You mean he was . . . he was smoking *opium*?

Raymond   You want me to spell it out?

Charles   I can't . . .

Raymond   Well, you'd better: you'd better wake up and believe it.

Charles   And I offered – I mean, you're *positive*?

Raymond   Bert Kowlaski's a notorious drug fiend. He's been fired from every circus from here to Arkansas. Notorious.

Charles   Oh dear.

Raymond   If you only knew.

Pause.

Charles   But I . . . I thought, I thought you didn't know him, Raymond?

Raymond   I don't know him, but I know *of* him. He's bad news and I suggest quite strongly that you stay clear of him until I can have a discreet word in Mervyn's ear.

Charles   Oh my! I didn't . . . and I . . . opium indeed. I've heard it sends people, heard it sends them . . .

Raymond   Insane?

Charles   Does it? In your, in your experience, Raymond? Does it send them – I mean, that could be dangerous. It could be dangerous: *insanity.*

Raymond   Not could, *is.*

Charles   Really?

Raymond   Yes. Insanity *is* dangerous.

Charles   And you think, you think –

Raymond (*pointing towards the bathroom*)   You need any more proof? The man's half demented already. You heard him going on and on and on about Wichita, ranting, ranting on and on about Wichita . . . the man's delusional, Charles, the man's delusional and the last thing Mervyn needs is delusional Munchkins on his production.

Charles   . . . You don't think it could make him turn, turn him and make him turn violent, do you?

Raymond   There's no telling with these fiends: violence is a possibility.

Charles   Oh dear.

Charles *sits down and shakes his head.* **Raymond** *pours him a glass of whisky and hands it to him.*

Raymond   Here. Drink this.

Charles   I don't really –

Raymond   It calms the nerves. Trust me.

Charles   Huh, but –

Raymond   Just drink it for heaven's sake.

Charles   You're sure, Raymond?

Raymond   Positive. Drink it.

Charles   I don't know.

Raymond   There is absolutely nothing *to* know.

Charles *takes a sip of the whisky and pulls a sour face.*

Raymond   It's less – take it back in one – it's less harsh if you take it back in one.

Charles *knocks the whisky back and coughs.* **Raymond** *has another ready for him.*

Charles   My word . . .

Bert *returns from the bathroom, climbs up on his bed and lies down.* **Charles** *eyes* **Bert** *suspiciously.*

Bert   Wake me up during the credits.

The door slowly opens. **Bert** *sits up,* **Charles** *and* **Raymond** *turn and stare.*

Philomena, *early twenties, smartly dressed – holding her outsized case – peeks her head round the door like a frightened rabbit.*

Raymond   . . . Yes? Can we . . . ?

Philomena (*furtively closing the door on herself*)   . . . I must have the wrong . . .

Bert (*laughing, shouting after her*)   Hey, wait a minute, honey, I got a itch needs scratching.

Bert *lies back and laughs to himself.* **Raymond** *shakes his head and pours* **Charles** *another shot.*

Raymond   Here.

Charles   No, really.

Raymond   My dear boy, you're going to have to develop a taste for whisky if you wish to hold on to your sanity.

Charles   Really?

Raymond   Oh yes.

Charles   Oh dear.

Raymond   Major productions are very stressful.

Charles   I feel a little . . . I feel queasy.

Raymond (*handing him the glass*)   You will, you will feel a little queasy. It's an acquired taste and you will feel a little . . . drink it.

Charles *reluctantly knocks the whisky back and grimaces.* **Raymond** *looks over at* **Bert**, *sleeping, and shakes his head.*

Raymond (*quietly*)   Just look at him, Charles, all the self-esteem of a sewer rat. Be sure to keep an eye on your valuables until I can arrange for his removal.

Charles   You'll be having words with Mer— Mr LeRoy?

Raymond   Strong words.

Charles   Yes?

Raymond   Oh yes. Very strong words.

Charles   About Mr – about Bert?

Raymond   Definitely, I'll definitely be having strong words in Mervyn's ear.

Charles (*holding his stomach*)   I can't see me acquiring a taste for it, Raymond.

Raymond (*pouring another glass*)   Nonsense, Charles . . . here.

Charles   No, no, I feel . . . I feel really . . .

The door opens. **Philomena** *sheepishly stands at the threshold, crying as a voice mocks:*

Booming male voice (*off*)   No mistakes, no mix-ups, honey, this is home. Don't worry, those little guys won't bother you. Hey, Harry, those little bastards got it made! Broads and everything . . .

Bert *groans in his sleep.* **Charles** *rushes into the bathroom, cupping his hands over his mouth.* **Raymond** *approaches* **Philomena**.

Raymond   Whatever seems to be the matter, young lady?

Philomena   . . . They . . . I . . . they say I've . . .

Philomena *breaks down.* **Raymond** *puts his arm around her and helps her in with her case.*

Raymond   What? They said what to you?

Philomena   . . . they say . . .

Raymond   The desk?

Philomena   . . . they say I've got to share this room . . .

Raymond   The desk said you've got to share *this* room?

Philomena   . . . they say there are no other rooms and that I've got to stay in here and share.

Her eyes flit hurriedly around the room, taking note of everything.

Raymond   *The desk* said this?

Philomena   I think so.

Raymond   Oh, I'm sure it's a mistake. They've got me down as a soldier on the call sheet. Oversights happen on productions of this scale.

Philomena   I, I don't –

Raymond   I'm the Mayor of Munchkinland and they've got me down as a soldier. Simple oversight, dear, nothing to worry about.

Offstage, we hear **Charles** *retching.* **Raymond** *and* **Philomena** *look over at the bathroom door.* **Bert** *groans and their attention is drawn to him.*

Raymond   We're expecting a *Mr* Kinsella. It's on the call sheet. It says Kinsella. *Mr* Kinsella.

Philomena *breaks down again, running to the chest of drawers and sobbing into it, her face turned away from them.* **Bert** *wakes up and watches them.*

Philomena   Kin . . . that's me. I'm Mr – I'm Kinsella. Philomena Kinsella . . . I just, I just want to go home. (*She turns round to face them.*) This is a mistake, I shouldn't, they said I shouldn't, I shouldn't have come here.

Raymond *picks up the call sheet and moves over to her.*

Raymond   I stand corrected. It doesn't say whether you're a male or female Kinsella, accept my apology.

Philomena   I'm not a man.

Raymond   No, no, it simply says Kinsella. No Philomena, no female, just Kins—

Philomena   Oh, this is just . . . it's all my fault. I shouldn't have come out here.

Raymond   Nonsense, whoever told you that? Don't worry your pretty little head, Miss Kinsella, I'll have a word with Mervyn, see if we can't find you female quarters.

Philomena   Mervyn?

Raymond   Just got off the phone with him.

Philomena   And, and this, this *Mervyn* can, he can get me another room?

Raymond   Mervyn *LeRoy*, Miss Kinsella. Mervyn *LeRoy* the producer.

Bert   Don't listen to him, honey. He's full o' shit. Used to be a big shot on the midget scene, now he's gonna be playing third fiddle in a troop o' Munchkin soldiers.

Raymond *glowers at* **Bert**.

Philomena (*to* **Bert**)   I shouldn't have come . . . this is awful . . . they told me, they said something awful would happen.

Bert   I'll take care of you, sweetie.

Raymond   Stay out of this, Kowalski.

Bert (*patting the bed*)   Climb up here, we can rehearse our lines together.

Raymond   Cut it out, Kowalski!

Bert   Can't blame me for trying, midgets get horny too, Ray . . . remember?

Bert *climbs down off the bed and goes to his case and rummages about in it, his back to the audience, clearly packing away his pipe.*
Raymond *leads* **Philomena** *to a chair and sits her down.*

Philomena   This is just awful.

Raymond   Now, now, Miss Kinsella. Nothing that can't be remedied.

Philomena   I can't . . . why would they want to – they know I'm not a man.

Raymond (*pouring a glass of whisky*)   Here, drink this, it'll calm your nerves.

Philomena   Thank you, but –

Raymond   No, please, I insist.

Charles *returns from the bathroom, looking decidedly ill. He is surprised by* **Philomena**'s *presence.*

Raymond   Charles, I'd like to introduce you to –

Bert   Our missing Munchkin's here, Charlie, and *he's* a fucken doll.

Raymond   This is Miss Kinsella, Charles. I was explaining to her that they've obviously made a mistake. I'll be having words with Mervyn, see if we can't find her some female quarters.

Charles *offers his hand to* **Philomena**. *They gently shake.*

Raymond   Charles is from your neck of the woods, Miss Kinsella. Now, what about the suggestion that we repair to the restaurant across the street before turning in? I don't know about anyone else but I'm famished.

Raymond *heads to the chest of drawers.* **Bert** *climbs down from the bed, then rubs his hands together.*

Bert   I heard the food's bad, but I don't listen to gossip.

Raymond *is looking on top of the chest and in his drawers for something. The cufflinks are gone.*

Charles   I don't know, will there be big people there?

Bert   Who you thinks gonna be waiting on us, Charlie?

Raymond   Everything will be in order and we'll all be quite safe. This I guarantee. Miss Kinsella?

Philomena   I'm not staying here by myself.

Raymond   Good, that's settled. Can't seem to find those cufflinks . . .

Raymond *has another search, then shrugs and goes into his case, produces a different set and puts them on.* **Charles** *pulls on his jacket.* **Bert** *is ready and clearly impatient.*

Bert: C'mon. Ray!

Raymond *looks suspiciously at* **Bert**, *then extends his arm in a loop and* **Philomena** *takes it. They exit as the lights go down.*

Scene Two

Bert, **Raymond**, **Charles** and **Philomena** *are sitting at an outsized table on outsized chairs in a restaurant. The large plates have been cleared and there are several huge wine bottles – all empty. The four big glasses each have a mouthful of wine left in them.*

Philomena   That was a wonderful meal. I don't know if I'll be able to sleep tonight after having eaten all that.

Charles   Yes, it was rather a lot.

Raymond   It's generally not a good idea to eat so much so late. Hard on the digestive system, you know. But I never have a problem sleeping, being a practitioner of the *Alexander Technique.*

Philomena   Thank you for making me feel so welcome, you've all been very kind. I didn't mean to become hysterical, it's just not what I expected . . . (*To* **Charles**.) You didn't think I was hysterical, did you? Sister Helena used to say I was hysterical . . . I'd hate to think I'd been hysterical in front of you.

Charles   No, no, no – not at all. I do think it's been rather a shock for all of us. It isn't every day that you're going to be a Munchkin in a Hollywood film! Such a beautiful spot as well. (*To the others.*) Did anyone see that wonderful silver birch tree in the courtyard at the back of the hotel?

Raymond   The fish was exquisite. I recall being in a Broadway production, some time ago – the name escapes me – there was a wonderful fish restaurant with equally exquisite fish. Have you been to New York, Miss Kinsella?

Philomena   We sailed into it but only had time to stay one night before we got put on a train. I'd have liked to have seen more of it. This is what's known as an 'Italian Restaurant', isn't it?

Bert   They got Italian joints where you come from?

Philomena   Joints?

Bert   Restaurants.

Philomena   Perhaps in Dublin, not in my town, no.

Bert   You're next door to Italy and you ain't got one?

Charles   I believe there are Italian Restaurants in London but I haven't come across one.

Bert   I reckon your King eats Italian food any time he likes, huh?

Charles   Well, I suppose if the King wanted to eat Italian food, he would just set sail to Italy.

Bert   Suppose if you're a king . . . or even a mayor, you get those privileges, hey, Ray?

Raymond   Are you trying to needle me again, Kowalski?

Bert   I'm just sayin some people get to eat anything they like. (*Lets out a loud belch.*)

Charles   Really, Bert. There's a lady present.

Philomena   Oh , I don't mind. I come from a family of eight. My brothers –

Bert   Don't get on no high horse here, Charlie, just cos you're a gardener to the fucken King. (*To* **Philomena** *and* **Raymond**.) You guys realise we're in the presence of royalty here?

Philomena   Royalty?

Charles   Well, I did have a gardening position at the Royal Gardens at Kew but I would hardly say . . .

Bert   Hear that, Philomena? If your bush ever needs to get trimmed, Charlie here's your man.

Philomena   What bush? What do you mean?

Bert   Forget it, honey. (*Shouts to floor.*) Hey there! (*Turns to others.*) Let's get that waiter over here with another bottle o' wine.

Charles   Keep your voice down! The big people might –

Bert   Big people my ass! You give them too much respect, Charlie!

Charles *sheepishly bows his head.*

Bert   Show 'em too much respect n' they walk all over you. Fucken bullies you want my opinion!

Raymond   Keep your voice down, Kowalski.

Charles   Actually, huh, Bert's got a point.. . . the big people I worked with in the gardens could be terrible bullies.

Bert   Yeah, right. Get some of those big cocksuckers in a mob, they start thinkin that you're put on this Earth for their fucken amusement. Right, Philomena?

Philomena   Goodness, no. They were all very kind in the village back home. (*Pause.*) Well, most of them were. Some of them gave us food. Then the nuns . . . the nuns picked me up and looked after me. Not all big people are bullies.

Bert   OK, but you're from the land o' the little people, right? Maybe us types get a better deal where you're from, honey.

Charles *recoils as if in memory.* **Raymond** *turns to him.*

Raymond   Does the name Jeffrey Hudson ring a bell?

Charles   Jeffrey . . . ?

Raymond   Jeffrey Hudson was a small person who was a retainer at the court of Charles I. 'The King's dwarf' they called him. He was born in Rutland, the smallest county in England, I believe. Motto: '*Multum in Parvo*' – *much in little*. He was probably one of the first small-people performers, a forerunner – in a crude way of course – to the thespians of today.

Bert   A fucken court jester!

Raymond   I'm sure that *you* would look at it like that.

Bert   What other way is there to look at it, Ray? He was
there to amuse the fucken King, like little Charlie here. Only
it wasn't even no king that Charlie had to amuse, it was that
mob o' green-fingered cocksuckers, right, Charlie?

Charles   I should never have left home, should never have
left my garden. I was safe at home. I thought I'd be taken
care of at Kew, but those big bullies – all I wanted was to be
left in peace to do my job of work – I . . .

Raymond   What you need to do with such people is give
them a taste of their own medicine.

Bert   You'd know all about that, Ray . . . Big Jim Murdock,
right?

Raymond   What are you, talking about, Kowalski?

Bert   Big Jim was the circus strongman with Fred Corelli,
back in Wichita, 'twenty-nine . . .

Raymond   I've told you, Kowalski. I –

Bert   Nice guy. Couldn't handle the sauce though. Turned
into a real mean bastard on the sauce. Like a different fucken
guy.

Charles *is looking uncomfortable.*

Bert   Know the type, Charlie?

Charles   Yes, the big gardeners . . . they . . . they . . .

Philomena *notes his distress and comforts him.*

Bert   Big Jim's been on the hooch all day playin cards and
I'm takin him and his buddies for the dumb schmucks they
are, cleanin those big assholes right out. Well, Jim gets sore
and he gets the notion that he's gonna throw some dwarf ass
around. Like see how far he can throw us . . .

Raymond   Kowalski . . .

Charles   They hung me upside down from a tree . . .

Philomena   No! Surely not. Never in the gardens of the King himself!

Bert   . . . We all had shit, Charlie, we all had shit. Thing is, instead of me, this asshole picks on Ray here, Ray with those fucken mitts like vices . . .

Raymond *is about to react to* **Bert** *when* **Philomena** *runs her hand up and down his arm.*

Philomena   Goodness! They *are* very strong arms. Feel the muscles in Raymond's arms, Charlie.

Raymond *flexes his muscles and smiles at* **Philomena**, *then looks half hopefully at* **Charles**.

Philomena   Go on, Charlie.

Charles   What?

Philomena   Feel his muscles.

Charles   I don't want to feel his muscles!

Bert   . . . So Ray grabs this cocksucker by the balls and won't let go till this asshole – this fucken *strong*man – starts squealin like a short-changed Times Square hooker.

Philomena *and* **Charles** *look at* **Raymond** *in admiration.*

Charles   Is that true, Raymond? You bested a big chap?

Bert   Not just a fucken *big chap*, Charles; that limp-wristed waiter faggot who won't bring over more fucken wine is a *big chap*. We're talkin Big Jim Murdock, who's as much a fucken giant to the likes of those waiter cocksuckers as they are to you. Wichita, 'twenty-nine, right, Ray?

Raymond   It's true that I have been known to stand up to bullies. It's also true that I do have an exceptionally strong grip. However . . . I am an actor and if truth be known I don't particularly like to dwell on my physical achievements. But . . . well, Kowalski, you seem intent on trying to needle me.

Raymond *grabs* **Bert**'s *hand and* **Bert** *prepares for a bout of arm-wrestling but* **Raymond** *starts to squeeze.* **Bert** *is clearly in some discomfort.*

Bert   Chrissakes, Ray –

Raymond   I have to say though, Mr Kowalski, that on this particular occasion you are mistaken . . .

Raymond *increases the pressure on* **Bert**'s *hand.*

Bert   I – fuck, Ray –

Raymond   . . . I wasn't in Wichita in nineteen twenty-nine.

Bert   OK! OK!

Raymond   Do you understand, Kowalski?

Bert   Yep, yep! Leggo my goddam –

Raymond   I'm so glad that we understand each other. It will make our stay together so much more civilised. Incidentally, you haven't seen a pair of gold cufflinks in the room, have you?

Bert   I don't know nothing bout no cufflinks –

Raymond   I'm sure you'd inform me if you came across them.

Bert   I would, I fucken would . . . please . . .

Raymond *releases his grip as* **Bert** *gasps and wrings out his hand.*

Bert   Jesus Christ . . .

Raymond   Now that this little misunderstanding has been cleared up, I must now turn my attention to getting myself more appropriately cast – and Miss Kinsella suitably billeted, of course.

Philomena   Oh, Raymond . . . you really think you'd be able to do that?

Raymond   Mervyn LeRoy I would count as – I would consider – and I can say this of perhaps only a handful of people in my acquaintance – as a close personal friend. I would also be failing in my duty if I stood by while an honourable and decent young lady (*looks to* **Bert**) was forced to remain in proximity to the morally questionable.

Philomena   Oh thank you, thank you so much, Raymond . . .

Raymond *sees something from the corner of his eye.*

Raymond   Waiter! Another bottle of wine if you please. Thank you. (*Turns again to* **Bert**.) There we are, Mr Kowalski. Civility and authority: tools of the trade for the thespian *and* the mark of a gentleman.

Charles   I think it's so marvellous that we're all going to be living together.

Raymond *raises his glass in toast.*

Raymond   To Hollywood!

Charles *and* **Philomena** – *with enthusiasm* – *and* **Bert** – *with reluctance – join in the toast.*

Act Two

The song 'Somewhere Over the Rainbow' starts to play.

The same hotel room, only a lot more 'lived in'. Clothes are strewn around, empty bottles of whisky litter the floor, beds are unmade and ashtrays are overflowing; it is clearly some weeks into the production.

Charles *enters dressed as a baby Munchkin. He looks around, then satisfied the room is empty, heads straight for a full bottle of Scotch on the table. He's clearly stressed out and in desperate need of a drink. He polishes off the whisky, pours another and repeats the process.*

Raymond, *wearing a Munchkin soldier uniform and carrying a wooden gun, enters tentatively, standing in the doorway.*

Charles *turns to face him, tense with rage and fear.*

Charles   Keep away from me!

Raymond   My dear boy, whatever's the matter?

Charles   What you did to me last night . . .

Raymond *shuts the door behind him. He takes a step forward.*

Raymond   It was for your own good . . . it was an old thespian trick, well utilised in theatrical circles in order to combat the –

Charles   You hurt me . . . I can hardly . . .

Raymond *steps forward.* **Charles** *steps back.*

Charles   Keep away from me, you . . . you beast!

Raymond *stops, moves back towards the door.*

Raymond   You caused the pain yourself by being so tense. I told you to relax. All functioning depends on the correct balance of tension in the entire neuromuscular system from head to toe. Granted, I normally practise this with other *actors*, skilled in the art of relaxation, the Alexander Technique . . . I forgot that the lay person often has difficulty . . . (*Stepping forward.*) Let me see what's wrong . . .

Charles, *snarling dementedly, charges forward a few paces and* **Raymond** *retreats, opening the door.*

Charles   FUCKING LEAVE ME ALONE!

Raymond   I'll let you simmer down, Charles . . . a most unseemly outburst.

He exits and shuts the door behind him.

Charles *makes for the whisky and pours himself another drink. Something catches his eye. His drawer in the chest is slightly open. He goes over and pulls it open. He rummages through the drawer in panic.*

Terrified, he starts looking around, under beds, pillows, mattresses, etc.

Philomena *enters dressed as one of the 'Lullaby League'. She is holding a yellow brick in her hand. She looks exhausted and immediately takes off her shoes.*

Philomena (*sitting down on the floor, massaging her feet*) . . . Half past four this morning I was on that set. Half past *four*! Sure, we didn't get a break until twelve. Miss Garland didn't come on set until ten and then she kept fluffing her lines and that horrible little dog kept peeing everywhere . . . managed to get a yellow brick though. Little memento. One of the labourers said it would be OK . . . What was all that noise last night? I didn't get to sleep until after twelve, and I had to get up at three thirty. Were you and Raymond arguing, Charlie? It sounded like you were arguing. It's not fair really, I mean it's really not fair. We should all learn to get on . . . are you . . . Charlie, are you listening to me?

Charles   . . . My . . . my money's gone. My wallet . . . I trusted him. We were all supposed to be Munchkins together. He did that to me, now my money's gone.

Philomena (*not listening to* **Charles**)   Oh, nearly forgot, I heard a rumour, well, it was the labourer, the labourer who gave me the yellow brick, he told me not to say anything, but . . . well, do you want to know or not, Charles?

Charles   Uh?

Philomena   Victor, Mr Fleming. He's leaving us to do a motion picture called *Gone With the Wind*. I can't wait to tell – what am I saying? Raymond'll probably know. There's not much gets past Raymond. The things Raymond doesn't know about this production aren't worth knowing. Sure, he told me that himself. He's a very wise man.

She looks over at **Charles** *and notices he is preoccupied.*

You're not listening, Charles. Charles, are you listening to me?

Charles   . . . My money, it's . . . it was, I left it in here, and now it's gone. I trusted him –

Philomena   Gone! It can't have just *gone*, it can't have gone . . . I hope you're not suggesting that someone in here . . . that it's just *gone*.

She puts the yellow brick on her bedside table and goes over to **Charles**.

You'll have only been misplacing it, Charles. Have another look. It can't have *gone*, money doesn't just go. Have another lo—

Charles (*breaking down and crying*)   I'm telling you it's fucking gone.

Philomena (*feigning shock*)   Well, there's no need for that kind of talk! (*Pause.*) Wait till Raymond gets here and talk to him. He'll know what to do.

Charles   Him . . . he's an evil, twisted liar! How would he know what to do! Did he get the part of Mayor from his 'friend' Mr LeRoy? Did he?

He grabs **Philomena** *by the shoulders and forces her to look around the room.*

Did he get you another room? Did he?

Philomena *pulls away from him.*

Philomena   Don't blame Raymond, he explained that he didn't want to put any pressure on his friend Mr LeRoy. I know you're upset about the money, but it can't have gone, it must just be mislaid, that's all. You've mislaid it.

Charles   It's not fucking mislaid. It's all I had, everything I had. How I am going to get home?

Philomena   Would you like me to have a look for you, Charles?

Charles *wipes at his eyes and pours another whisky.*

Charles   I'm stuck here . . . I'm stuck here like that stupid little bitch in Oz.

Philomena   Please! You'd make a stevedore blush, Charles Merryweather, you really would. You've been spending too much time around that horrible Bert Kowalski . . . I'll have a look for you.

Charles (*yelling*)   ARE YOU DEAF?

Philomena   There's no need to be . . . You might want to be askin your 'good friend' Mr Kowalski if he knows of your money's whereabouts if you insist that it's 'gone'.

Charles   Bert's a good friend of mine. Bert wouldn't – just stay out of this.

Philomena   Very well, be like that. See if I care, I was only trying to help . . . and besides, if it has 'gone' it'll have 'gone' on liquor that you've forgotten about.

Charles   I haven't forgotten about liquor! Just . . . just leave me alone.

Philomena (*looking around at the mess*)   And if you think I'm cleaning this room up *again*, you've got another thing coming. I'm an actress not a bloody chambermaid.

Philomena *picks up her make-up box and marches into the bathroom indignantly.* **Charles** *sits sobbing into the whisky.* **Bert** *enters dressed as a 'Lollipop Kid'. He is smoking a very large cigar and is full of himself.* **Charles** *quickly wipes at his tear-stained face and tries to act normal. Offstage, we hear the bath taps running.*

Bert   . . . What a guy. Victor Fleming. Victor Fleming's some guy! If this picture don't break all box-office records I'll shave my ass in Times Square . . . Got talking to Mervyn at lunch, told him how much I enjoyed *Fugitive from a Chain Gang*, offered me a part in his next picture, he's calling it *Quo Vadis*. Great title, beats me the fuck what it *means*, but, eh, beggars can't be choosy . . . That fucken leprechaun in the tub again?

Charles *nods his head in positive.*

Bert   Fucken pussy of hers must stink like Docherty's Pig time she spends in that tub. Should be careful she don't wash that little Irish ass away.

He notices **Charles***'s downbeat mood.*

'Sup with you, you need your diaper changing or something?

He picks up a bottle of whisky and pours the last drops out of it. He knocks back the whisky and sighs.

You fancy eating out at the diner tonight, Charlie?

Charles   I've no . . . I'm short –

Bert   No sweat, it's on me, cleaned the Cowardly Lion out at lunch. Told him, said: 'Never mind asking the Wizard for courage; when you get to the Emerald City, you just ask him to teach you how to play craps, you schmuck.' You should join us sometime, Charlie. They're *good* people . . . Garland let me sit on her lap today . . . gee, I had me one hell of a fucken boner, she must o' noticed, put me down real fast, must o' thought I was gonna toss my cookies right there and then. What I wouldn't give to stick my head up that gingham dress and munch away on that sweet apple pie o' hers . . . (*Looks to* **Raymond***'s bed.*) . . . That fucken pain in the ass not been back yet?

Charles *winces and shakes his head in the negative.*

Bert   So whaddayasay?

Charles   What do I say about what?

Bert   Play our cards right, might even pick up some *Munchkin pussy.* I heard those two Dutch dwarfs sucked just about every cock in Culver City, coroner reckons they're partial to a toot or two on the white stuff . . . but you know me, Charlie, I don't listen to gossip . . .

He pulls out a little bottle and winks at **Charlie**.

. . . Cocaine. Cost me a pretty penny . . . can't see the attraction myself, if I wanted to get paranoid I'd compare dick sizes with the Scarecrow, got a pecker on him the size o' Philomena . . . So whaddayasay?

He looks around the floor for a bottle with any whisky left in it.

'S'bout time that *cocksucker* put his hand in his pocket. He's putting the bite on every fucken midget here, owes the Mayor fifteen bucks, even tried to tap up the Wicked Witch o' the West for a five I heard . . . When's that fucken leprechaun gonna start cleaning this place up! If she didn't spend so much time soaping up that stinking pussy o' hers . . .

He lights up his cigar and looks across at **Charles**. **Charles** *has his head bowed.*

. . . You know she ain't really no dwarf. She was once five ten, she's just fucken *shrunk* on account o' all the time she spends in the tub . . . What's eating you, Charlie?

Charles   Nothing . . . I just . . . I want to . . . I just want to go home, Bert.

Bert   As little miss cock-tease herself says: 'There's no place like home.'

Charles   I need to –

Bert   You want my advice, you stay away from that fucken cocksucker Ray if you want my advice. Guy's trouble. Guy's getting himself a name, I hear things, people are talking about him. I knew, knew it wouldn't be no time 'til people started talking 'bout him, knew it wouldn't be no time at all 'til Ray got himself a *name*. I could – I mean – if I was like that, if I was that way *induced* I could tell you things about that cocksucker.

Charles   Some of the chaps on the set have been talking, Mr Taylor included, about living in California together, after the filming. Down in San Diego. There's even talk that an architect is building houses for little people! Do you think we could get one, Bert?

Bert   That's all a cocksucking *myth*. Don't believe that kinda bullshit, Charlie. I heard it all before, a nice community for little people. Houses for little people! Wise up, kid! Hell's gonna get a cold snap before they build houses for the likes of us.

Charles *looks cut to the quick.*

Charles   Oh my, I really hoped . . . I need to get out of here.

Bert   Reckon the way it's going, one more week we should be –

Charles   A week?

Bert   A week the very *least* is all.

Charles *shoots over to* **Bert**.

Bert   What?

Charles (*gripping hold of* **Bert***'s lapels, pleading*)   No, no, a week! No, that's no good. A week's no good, I need –

Bert   Woah, take it easy, take it easy, Charlie.

Charles   This place is *evil*, Bert. It's evil. I need to get out. I need to get away right now!

Bert   Hey, *evil's* a little over the top. Sure, they've got to calling this place Babylon Heights but I think you're maybe overreacting here a little.

Charles   I can't – I just can't face it any more.

Bert   Face it? Face fucken what? You can't face me and you suckin down on juicy sirloins and quarts o' bourbon, maybe getting our dicks *sucked* by those two Dutch honeys later, uh?

Charles   No, it's, it's not that.

Bert   You gotta – look, you gotta calm down, Charlie, I'll go down the liquor store, uh? Get us a drink, OK? You just need to calm down a little. Here, come on, lie down, uh, have a nap, Hollywood's got a way o' getting to little people.

Charles   . . . I really need to get out, Bert.

Bert   Yeah, yeah, sure you do, kid. You need – we all need to get out. You get a nap, you get a nap and I'll get us a drink, OK?

Bert *leads* **Charlie** *over to the bed.* **Philomena** *comes out of the bathroom, a towel over her hair and a long dressing gown buttoned up to her neck. She glowers at* **Bert**.

Philomena   I heard every word, Mr Kowalski, and there is absolutely nothing *unsavoury* about my va . . . If you must know, the only reason I take regular baths is because they relax me. Unlike you I don't need alcohol and opium to make me feel comfortable and if you are planning on having a word with Mr LeRoy would you please kindly tell him that I've got a few words for him regarding your own disgusting behaviour . . . and, and, and if you must know, the reason Charlie wants to get out of here is because he's sick of being corrupted by you, you've turned him from a decent young man into a nervous wreck.

Bert   You finished?

Philomena   May God have mercy on your black soul.

Philomena *grabs a hold of a chair and climbs up on to her bed.*

Bert (*helping* **Charles** *up on to the bed*)   How's about you
letting me sniff that pussy o' yours you're so confident it don't
reek, Philomeany?

Philomena (*yelling*)   I hope you burn in hell, you odious
little animal!

Bert   Quit playing hard to get, honey.

Philomena *pulls the covers over her head.* **Bert** *laughs as he lays*
Charles *on the bed and climbs down from it.*

Charles   . . . How am I going to get home, Bert? I wish
. . . When do we get paid, Bert? Will they pay me now? If
I . . . will they pay me if I ask them now, Bert?

Bert   Just calm down. You'll get paid, don't worry about
getting paid, Charlie. They're cocksuckers, OK, they suck
cock but they're MGM cocksuckers; they're not gonna
welch on paying Munchkins. That's the kind o' publicity they
don't need. You imagine – just picture it: two hundred
Munchkins rioting in Hollywood, midgets running fucken riot
in the hills is the kind of publicity they don't need right now.
Think about it: bad for business . . . and besides, Louis B.
Mayer's a fucken dwarf f'chrissakes. He won't see us get
fucked over.

Charles   . . . You spoke to . . . Bert, you said you spoke to
Mr LeRoy?

Bert   Uh-huh.

Charles   That's good.

Bert   Mighty fucken civil you ask me. I spoke to him. The
guy listens.

Charles   Well . . .

Bert   You got a point you wanna get to?

Charles   Look, look . . .

Bert   I'm looking, I'm looking.

Charles   . . . something . . . something *has* . . .

Bert   Go ahead, I'm all ears. I'm all ears from my ass to my halo, friend like you wants to talk: go ahead.

Charles   Thank you, Bert.

Bert   You're welcome.

Charles   I've . . .

Bert   You need a good drink inside you. What you need inside you they sell at the liquor store under the counter round the back away from fucken weasly eyes.

Charles   I don't . . . listen . . .

Bert   You need a bottle o' bourbon in you.

Charles   Don't – please don't say *that*.

Bert   Then fuck the bourbon I'll get malt.

Charles   Just – could you, just until they pay me, could you ask him if I can, if they'll put me in another . . .

Charles *starts to weep again.*

Bert   What? . . . Go on, Charlie? What do you want? What do you want me to ask Merv?

Pause.

Charles   . . . No . . . nothing, Bert . . . I can't, I don't want you to ask him anything. I can't –

Bert   Anything.

Charles *buries his head in the pillow.* **Bert** *ponders for a while then makes for the door.*

Bert   I'll go get us something to drink, Charlie. Calm you down, OK? I'll get us a bottle to calm you down, right?

Bert *exits.* **Charles** *climbs down and goes and stands at the side of* **Philomena***'s bed. He reaches up and tugs on her leg.*

Charles   Please . . . Philomena, wake up, Philomena.

Philomena *sits up.*

Philomena (*angry*)   I wasn't asleep.

Charles   I'm sorry, Philomena.

Philomena   What do you want, Charles?

Charles   I'm sorry for, I need to . . . Philomena, have you any money you could loan me? I'll wire it to you as soon as I get home, I promise –

Philomena   You've got to be kidding, Charles! Loan you money, loan you money so you can buy more liquor and opium!

Charles   No, no, I won't – I've got to get away from here. I'll make sure you get my pay, you can have it, have it all, I don't want it . . . I just want to go home. I'll wire you –

Philomena   I haven't got any money to give you, and if I did I wouldn't. You didn't listen to me, I told you time and time again to stay away from that *monster* but you wouldn't listen to *me*. Mr Benedict-Porter . . . Raymond . . . was right –

Charles   Don't! Don't talk about that . . . I can't . . . I just need to go home.

Philomena   I'm sorry for you, Charles, I really am, but sure you've got to learn . . . Will you look at yourself. You're a wreck, Charles Merryweather. That's what alcohol and opium does to people . . . I didn't hear you – why didn't you ask Kowalski? You didn't ask him for money, did you? You should have asked him for your money back!

Charles   He won it from the Cowardly Lion.

Philomena   You don't believe that, do you? You don't seriously – you don't believe the Cowardly Lion would seriously have anything to do with an *animal* like Kowalski?

Charles   He's not an animal!

Philomena   I've worked with animals and I'm telling you he *is*.

Charles   Bert's good to me. He *listens*.

Philomena   *I* listen. Mr Benedict-Porter listens. That's all we ever do. All we ever do is listen to you, Charles. It's you that doesn't listen . . . if you, if you listened you'd know that.

Charles   I just . . . I just want to go home.

Philomena   You should have thought about that. You should have thought about going home before you decided not to listen to us.

Philomena *lies down and pulls the covers over her head.* **Charles** *breaks down and starts to cry.*

Charles   Please, Philomena. I know . . . I know you've got money. I'll . . . I promise I'll wire it to you.

Philomena   No, Charles. No, it's for your own good. Now –

Charles   But –

Philomena   That's my last word, I need some sleep.

Charles (*yelling at her*)   YOU'RE A MEAN FUCKING LITTLE WITCH!

Philomena *sits up, at the end of her tether.*

Philomena   You won't manage to drag me down to your and Kowalski's level, Charles Merryweather, I'll tell you that now! Never!

She pulls the covers over her head. **Charles** *staggers over towards his bed. He suddenly stops and grabs at his stomach. He slowly delves under his baby romper, pulls off the diaper and wraps a towel around his waist. He inspects the diaper. It is covered in blood. He drops it to the floor and runs crying into the bathroom like a man possessed.* **Charles** *slams the door shut.*

Philomena *sits up. She looks across at the bloody diaper on the floor, climbs out of bed and goes to it. She is puzzled as she gingerly picks it up by a corner. She walks over to the bathroom door and knocks on it.* **Charles** *can be heard sobbing in the bathroom.*

Philomena   Charles, what's wrong? . . . What's wrong, Charles? You should go see the doctor if you're passing blood, it could . . . it could be serious, Charles. It's not healthy and you should go see the doctor . . .

She knocks harder.

. . . Your nappy's full of . . . it's covered in *blood*, Charles. Do you hear me, Charles? I don't want to alarm you but your nappy's full of blood . . . please, let me – come out of there. Now. (*Pause.*) I'm . . . I'm sorry I told you to . . . Charles, Charlie. Listen, Charles. It could be, I think, it could be your drinking. You're drinking far too much. Don't say I didn't warn . . . Look, forget what I said, I didn't mean it, Charles. I'm really tired. I didn't mean what I said, but you should have listened to me. I knew it would all end in . . .

She stares at the blood-soaked diaper.

. . . This is what happens when you don't listen to people. When you don't listen to people and you end up passing blood through your back passage into your nappy like that *animal*, Kowalski.

Charles (*off*)   Lend me some money, Philomena! I'm begging you. I. Am. Begging. You. To. Lend. Me. Some. Money!

Philomena   Money's not going to solve anything, you hear, just come out, come out and we'll talk about –

Charles (*off*)   I just want – I need to go home.

Philomena   Sure I'll go to the doctor's with you myself if you're ashamed. If you're ashamed about the . . . I'll go with you. It's the least I can do, Charlie.

Long pause. **Charles** *can be heard sniffling. He comes to the door.*

Charles   Why . . . ?

Philomena (*sighing*)   What? Why what?

A pause. **Charles** *walks over to where the diaper is. He picks it up and puts it in a drawer.*

What? Why? Talk to me.

Charles   . . . Why won't you lend me the money to go home?

Philomena   Because – that isn't the issue here, Charles. The issue here is the blood in your nappy and your drinking. Money's not the issue, the issue's your . . . money's not going to solve anything . . . what you need –

Charles (*yelling pathetically*)   JUST LEND ME THE FUCKING MONEY! THAT'S WHAT I NEED, I NEED MONEY TO GET HOME!

Philomena *seethes. She is about to yell back at him but she counts down her anger and tries a calm approach.*

Philomena   I'm trying to . . . Look, Charles, I'm trying to help you.

She puts an arm around him and leads him to his bed. He lies down, whimpering softly.

If you're ashamed, it's nothing to be – I'll go to the doctor. I'll go out of my way and bring him back, I'll bring the doctor back to you to look at your back passage.

Charles   *No!* I don't need a doctor. Just . . . just stay with me. Stay with me in case he comes back.

Charles *cries softly, as* **Philomena** *lies alongside him, hugging him.*

Philomena   Oh, that evil man Kowalski, he's really hurt you by giving you all that drink and opium. You an innocent as well . . .

Charles   It's not Bert . . . it's that horrible Raymond . . .
(*Pause.*) Do you think that they will have a special place where
all Munchkins, all little people can go and live together?

Philomena   Sure they will, Charles, I've heard it said. I'm
going to save up and buy a little house with a big lock on the
door.

Charles   And I can come and stay with you?

Philomena   Sure, if you want to, Charles, but wouldn't
you like a place of your own?

Charles *considers this.*

Philomena   But you can stay with me if you want, Charles
. . . (*She strokes his face.*) . . . Skin as soft as a baby. Sure, that's
what you are, you're my little baby boy.

She starts to sing.

  While goin' the road to sweet Athy, hurroo, hurroo
  While goin' the road to sweet Athy, hurroo, hurroo
  While goin' the road to sweet Athy,
  A stick in me hand and a drop in me eye,
  A doleful damsel I heard cry,
  Johnny I hardly knew ye.

Charles *is lulled and succumbs, sucking his thumb like a child.*

Philomena   Do you like it when we hold each other like
this, Charles?

Charles   Yes.

Philomena   I thought you might. You men are all the
same. It feels nice, doesn't it?

Charles   Yes.

She starts to caress him, his head, shoulders and arms.

Philomena   You know what I used to do to men back
home, to men I liked? Men that were kind to me?

Charles   Big men?

Philomena   Men of all sizes, Charles. All sizes. I used to be able to make them feel nice. Wouldn't you like to feel nice, Charles?

She moves down his body, slowly kissing his chest, then moving under the sheets. He is in increasing discomfort as she kisses his stomach, pulling aside the towel.

Charles   NO! STOP IT!

Philomena *stops, pulls back, raising her head. She looks up at him in shock.*

Philomena   Jaysus! Where's . . . what happened to your boy thing, Charlie!

Charles *squeals, jumps out of the bed with the towel around him and pulls on his clothes.*

Philomena   Charlie –

Charles   Why do people always touch me? . . . WHY CAN'T YOU ALL LEAVE ME ALONE?!

Philomena *gets up from the bed with her gown fastened.*

Philomena   I'm going to get a doctor. You're not right, Charles Merryweather, all I wanted to do was make you feel better –

Charles   NO! I'LL NEVER BE BETTER!

He runs out, slamming the door behind him. **Philomena** *climbs up to the phone and picks it up, dialling the desk.*

Philomena   Hello . . . it's room two-two-four. It's Charles . . . Mr Charles Merryweather in two-two-four. He's . . . there's blood coming out of . . . he's . . . not right . . . he needs a doctor. (*Pause.*) But where is the doctor? (*Pause.*) Room two-two-four. (*Pause.*) No, he's not in the room now, no, he just left. (*Pause.*) I don't know . . . (*Pause.*) I'll go and find him then call you back.

She climbs down and takes her clothes into the bathroom to get dressed. Seconds later, **Bert** *enters holding a bottle of whisky in a brown bag.*

*He is barely in the door before he starts to screw off the top of the bottle. He kicks the door shut and looks around, seeing **Philomena**'s shoes on the bed.*

Bert   You hiding somewhere, Charlie, uh?

He hears noises coming from the bathroom.

Still in the fucken tub! I don't believe this shit!

He crashes on his bed and unscrews the bottle again, taking a slug.

Jesus fucken Christ. You must be the cleanest leprechaun that ever lived . . . either that or the dirtiest one, huh? You washin' your sins away, Philomeany?

Philomena *comes into the room with a hateful expression on her face, pointedly ignoring **Bert**. She locates her shoes and sits on the bed, focusing on lacing them up. **Bert** shrugs and takes another long pull on the whisky. He savours the taste.*

Bert   . . . Bet you spent a lotta time in the tub back in Ireland washing all that nun pussy. What a fucken job! If there's any vacancies in that line of work, you be sure to vouch for your old buddy Bert Kowalski, you hear.

Philomena *ignores him.* **Bert** *kicks off his shoes. He takes another long pull on the whisky.*

Bert (*looking over at **Charles**'s drawer*)   . . . the hell's Charlie gone, you freaky fucken leprechaun?

Bert *lights a cigarette.* **Philomena** *heads to the door, exiting, just as* **Raymond** *furtively enters, obviously unnerved a little by her abrupt departure. He closes the door and surveys the room.*

Raymond   No doubt you've been upsetting her again. Where's she gone?

Bert   Little witch was treatin me like I was fucken invisible.

Raymond   A highly understandable strategy, sadly deployed a little too late . . . (*Looks around the room in disgust.*) . . . This really isn't on. Just look at this room. It's a *pigsty*. There'd be hell, hell to pay if the desk saw this room.

Bert   All I care the desk can go fuck itself.

Raymond *winces in distaste as he goes to his bed, takes off his hat and undoes his jacket. He picks up an empty bottle of whisky and shoots a glance at* **Bert**.

Raymond (*picking up a glass*)   Um, could I? I mean, would you mind?

Bert (*offering him the bottle*)   Why change the routine, uh?

Raymond   Thank you.

Raymond *pours himself a large glass of whisky and keeps a hold of the bottle.* **Bert** *clicks his fingers and makes a gesture.* **Raymond** *reluctantly hands* **Bert** *the bottle back.*

Bert   You see Charlie on your way in?

Raymond   Charles?

Bert   Yeah, Charlie. You see him?

Raymond   No, why?

Bert   Why, why because he's got fucken cabin fever, that's why.

Raymond   Oh . . . ?

Raymond *climbs up on to a chair and starts to take off his boots.*

Bert   Kid wants to go home. Told him to hang in. He sure is edgy.

Raymond   Edgy?

Bert   You know . . .

Raymond   It happens.

Raymond *sighs heavily and takes another measured sip of whisky.*

Bert   How's army life?

Raymond   You won't . . . look: oversight, OK? I keep telling you it was a simple mistake. A slip-up in casting: some scatterbrain secretary making a hash of the call sheets and you won't let it . . . I've told you, I won't add to Mr LeRoy's hectic work schedule. I value our friendship too much to have him worrying about one little oversight.

Bert   You're all fucken heart, Ray. You know that? *All* heart. When it comes time for burying you, Ray, when that day comes they're gonna put you in a specimen jar, gonna bury you in a specimen jar cos you're all heart, Ray.

He climbs down off the bed. He sees the yellow brick on top of **Philomena**'s *locker. He picks it up. He takes it with him back to his bed, holding it up to the light, examining it.*

He was shakin' like a goddam leaf, sweatin like Philomeany's pussy, the poor fuck. White as a ghost, fucken DTs you ask me.

Raymond   Charles?

Bert   Charlie, yeah. That's right. Must o' – probably couldn't wait.

Bert *puts the brick down and shakes his head.* **Raymond** *twiddles with his empty glass.* **Bert** *goes to him and pours him a shot.*

Raymond   I meant to pick a bottle up on the way in.

Bert   Yeah, right . . . you seen the Mayor today?

Raymond   What if I did?

Bert   Asked me to remind you about that loan.

Raymond (*snapping*)   Not that it's any of your business, but I paid him back this afternoon.

Bert   Hey, just passing the message on. I'm just the messenger all right? I get a fucken *message* from the Mayor it's my *business*, OK?

Raymond   Point taken . . . You said Charles was . . . he seemed irate?

Bert   Irate? He seemed pissed is what he seemed. But irate, yeah, guess you could say irate.

Raymond   I think he's hysterical.

Bert   Like earlier?

Raymond   No, no, no, Kowalski, I wasn't *particularising*, you understand. I just think that his condition in *general* is *hysterical*.

Bert   Edgy, irate, pissed, hysterical, it's all the same shit. Kid's gone anyway.

Raymond   Gone where though?

Bert   I dunno. To get some liquor or to get his cock sucked by one of them Dutch broads, or to join some crap game. What does anybody do round here? Anyways, he'll be back.

Raymond   You know he doesn't set foot outside of this room other than to work unless he's accompanied by you, Kowalski. You know how nervous he is. I tried to tell him about your pernicious influence, attempted to provide adult guidance to an impressionable young man. I think that you've debauched him, and I'm going to call the desk to inform them of his state of mind.

Bert   You do that.

Raymond   I intend to. To let them know of his *hysterical* state of mind.

Bert   You're gonna call them, huh?

Raymond   . . . The desk will know who to contact. The desk will have *procedure* for this kind of thing.

Bert   This kind o' thing? The desk'll have things?

Raymond   Quite. Procedures.

Bert   'Procedures' for *hysteria*? The desk'll have 'procedures' for *hysterical midgets*, Ray?

Raymond   Medical procedures. They will have a local doctor they can contact; somebody who'll be able to give Charles something to calm him down.

Bert   He just needs a drink, or maybe even a little smoke.

Raymond   This is what all this is about, isn't it, Kowalski. A young boy – a *sensitive* boy – has been driven hysterical by your *debauchery*, and *your* only concern is that the desk remains unaware of your *nefarious* practices.

Bert *looks towards the bag that contains his pipe and his opium stash.*

Bert   C'mon, Ray, gimme a break –

Raymond   I'm no snitch, Kowalski, but as a professional I am duty-bound to put the well-being of a colleague and a member of this cast above the concealment of your dubious and highly illegal personal habits.

Bert *looks around at the empty whisky bottles.*

Bert   This stuff . . . you drank as much of this stuff as me, Ray, this *illegal* stuff.

Raymond   I doubt whether any local sales clerk would testify in court that I was the one who purchased these bottles of Scotch.

Bert *sits upright and points angrily at* **Raymond**, *denouncing him.*

Bert   No they wouldn't, you cocksucker! They couldn't. Cos *purchase* is the last fucken thing you'll do! It ain't gonna stop you fucken *drinkin*; it ain't gonna stop your fake-ass Ivy League mouth from wrappin itself round the neck of any bottle some other stiff's spent his hard-earned dimes on, it ain't gonna stop you doin that!

Raymond   I'm giving you a chance, Kowalski, a chance, you hear: a chance to clear up this evidence before I call the desk.

Bert   You two-faced asshole! You drank the shit; you clean up the mess!

Raymond *picks up the phone.*

Raymond   I'm calling the desk.

Bert   . . . You remember Muzzy Starr, Ray?

Raymond   What?

Bert   Muzzy Starr. Sure you do, sure you remember him, Ray.

Raymond   What is this? I've never heard of – (*Into phone.*) . . . Desk? Yes, Mr Benedict-Porter, no, no, no, don't put me on ho—

Bert   Muzzy Starr, Ray. He's around, he's around San Francisco right now. Right now he's around there getting his raggedy little ass shot out a fucken cannon.

Raymond *is trying to contain his ire.*

Raymond   Is there, a-are you trying to say *something* to me, Kowalski? Because if you are – if you are trying to say *something* to me –

Bert   Wichita, 'twenty-nine. Muzzy was, what? sixteen, seventeen? In 'twenty-nine Muzzy was seventeen, sixteen, uh?

Raymond   We've been through this. I thought I'd made it abundantly clear that I have never set foot in *Wichita*!

Bert   Muzzy's got proof you set foot in Wichita.

Raymond   Look –

Bert   Muzzy's got a ripped asshole and fucked-up insides proves you set foot in Wichita. Little fella's been shitting in a bag since then. Proof, Ray, proof: ripped ass and fucked-up insides. You know what else he's got, Ray? Witnesses. He's got witnesses too. You remember the Bearded Lady, uh? Nothing much got past that big ol' hairy bitch in Wichita, Ray.

Raymond *seethes and slams the phone down.*

Raymond   Have you – is that it? The dope's eaten your brain, you've *finally* –

Bert   He's got *proof*, Ray. Muzzy's got all the *proof* he needs. You think I'm fucken *dumb*, Ray? You take me for some dumb fucken schmuck or something?

Raymond I've never *heard* of this –

Bert He's a phone call away. That poor little fuck's been searching high and low for you, Ray.

Raymond You're insane!

Bert Insane, uh?

Raymond (*picking up the phone*) Quite, you're quite insane, Kowalski. Now I'm going to call the desk, I'm going to call the desk about poor Charles's drink- and opium-induced hysterical condition.

Bert Gimme a fucken break, Ray, they'll probably turn a blind eye to the booze, but if they find my stash –

Raymond *looks towards the bathroom.*

Raymond Flush it away, Kowalski.

Bert Ain't you ever had no break before?

Raymond I don't go poisoning impressionable young men with drugs.

Bert No, no, you go around fucking dwarfs in the *ass*.

Raymond *What!*

Raymond *climbs down to the floor.*

Bert Muzzy Starr, Ray. He's got witnesses, like me and you he's *got* witnesses.

Raymond For the last *time* –

Bert Guy comes to you, guy can't take a shit, you tell some guy you can cure him, you cure him all right, Ray. You stick your big fat hairy cock in his little ass*hole* and some guy never *stops* shitting.

Raymond How – I can't – you've got a diseased mind, Kowalski. You're diseased! It's the alcohol and the drugs. There's help available, you know. There are people that can help you, Kowalski.

Bert   Bearded Lady told me all about it. That big ol' hairy bitch marked your card, Ray. She tells me and I bump into Muzzy Starr outside Reno one night. Get him stoned he tells me everything. He tells me the *gory* details, Ray. You know I ain't one for gossip, but – Jesus – that poor kid. The thing you done to that poor little – fuck, Ray, I mean . . .

Raymond   Have you finished – for the last time – have you finished, Kowalksi?

Bert   You're not denying it, right? You're not saying you didn't *fuck* his ass with your cock, Ray?

Raymond   What's the point? What *is* the point? . . . you're wearing me down.

Bert   Bearded Lady, Muzzy Starr's witness, right . . . she . . . she reckons she could o' got you work, Ray . . . could o' got you work as a sideshow freak.

Raymond   Carry on, Kowalski, carry on indulging yourself.

Bert   That *schlong* you got on you.

Raymond   This is –

Bert   That right, is it, Ray? That right you got a . . . said you had a – said you was hung like a fucken horse. You're not denying it? You ain't denying you got a pecker on you size of a baby's arm, Ray?

Raymond *stands up, shakes his head and goes to the chair to climb back up to the phone.*

Bert   . . . She, the Bearded Lady, she said you weren't no fucken dwarf when it came down to your *dick*, Ray.

Raymond   I'm calling the desk, you're sick, Kowalski. Maybe I was wrong. Perhaps you're past the point of help, with your, your *delusional* nonsense. But I'm damned if I'm going to let poor Charles go the same way.

Raymond *starts to climb up.*

Bert   No desk, Ray, no desk. Think about it. I know things, Ray, don't be calling no desk.

Raymond   Shut up – will you just shut your mouth one minute.

Bert   No desk. Don't you dare you, you – hold it right there.

Raymond   What? What are you going to do if I don't hold it right here?

Bert *goes over to the chair.* **Raymond** *climbs down and they face each other.*

Bert   You fucked Muzzy Starr in his ass, you fucked him in his ass with that *schlong* you got and I don't hear you denying it. Muzzy's a big guy now, Ray. Last count he was three feet six. You know what else Muzzy Starr is, Ray?

Raymond   A *liar?*

Raymond *suddenly grabs* **Bert** *around the throat. He starts throttling him.* **Bert** *can barely breathe.*

Raymond   Now, now, now you listen . . . you listen to me *now*, Kowalski. Just you listen to me for one goddam minute . . .

Bert's *eyes bulge as he tries to gasp in acquiescence.*

Bert   . . . OK . . . you're choking . . . OK . . .

Raymond   *Choke you?* I should kill you, you sick – now listen to me, *listen.*

Bert   . . . OK . . . listening . . . let go . . .

Raymond *releases his grip.* **Bert** *is rubbing his neck and gasping for air.*

Raymond   This nonsense, this delusional nonsense has gotten out of hand.

Bert   OK. Just don't –

Raymond   The things, those sick things you're saying,
listen to me, you fool, are you listening to me?

Bert   I'm listening.

Raymond   You better *listen*, Kowalski, you better listen to
me . . . Now: Muzzy Starrs and Bearded Ladies, Wichita
'twenty-nine and constipation cures. I don't know anything
about all that, all right?

Bert *looks away.* **Raymond** *pokes him in the chest.* **Bert** *flinches.*

Raymond   Do you hear me, Kowalski? Do you hear what
I'm saying about non-existent Bearded Ladies and
constipation?

Bert   I hear you, I hear you –

Raymond   Raymond. Say it, I want to hear you say
Raymond.

Bert   . . . Ray . . . Raymond.

Raymond   Look at you, Kowalski, you sick drug fool.

Bert   You're a fucken *bully*, you know that.

Raymond *shoots to* **Bert** *and pulls his hand back.* **Bert** *crouches
against the wall in a pathetic defensive heap.*

Raymond   Why *you* –

Bert   OK, OK, I'm sorry, I'm sorry, OK?

Raymond (*pacing about*)   . . . Not a word of this, Kowalski.
Not a word, you hear? Not *one word* and I keep my mouth
shut about your dope.

Bert   Leave my dope out o' this.

Raymond   That's what I'm saying. I'm saying I'll leave
your dope out of this. You've no proof, you've nothing to
suggest –

Offstage, raised voices coming from the corridor.

Raymond   You've no proof I've ever set foot in Wichita, you, you and this mythical Muzzy – this mythical Bearded Lady, I mean, a Bearded Lady for heaven's sake!

Raymond *is distracted by noises coming from outside.*

Bert (*quietly to himself*)   They ain't mythical, they're unmythical, they're shittin n' pissin unmythical witnesses and they got proof you stuck your dick in his little asshole –

Bert *spots something on the floor; he follows a trail to* **Charles***'s drawer.* **Raymond** *watches him.*

Raymond   What on earth are you doing now? You really are in a terrible mess, Kowalski!

Bert   Look, look here. Shit looks like blood or something.

Raymond (*following the trail*)   *Blood*?

Bert   Sure looks like blood or shit or something.

Raymond   Make your mind up for heaven's sake.

Bert   OK, *blood*, it's fucken – looks like *blood*.

Raymond   It could be, ah, you know . . .

Bert   No, I don't know –

Raymond   Women's *problems*. You know, down below. She could be menstru—

Bert   She don't strike me the kind o' broad that'd just *bleed* all over some hotel.

There are more noises outside in the corridor. Raised voices, doors slamming.

Raymond   What – what's all that noise?

Bert   Noise? What *noise*?

Raymond   Out – in the corridor, the noise out in the corridor.

Bert   How'd I know? You think I'm *psychic*, uh?

Raymond   *Listen!*

Bert   You think I can see through walls or something? I'm no psychic.

Raymond   I know what it means, Kowalski. I know what *psychic* means and it doesn't mean you can see through *walls*.

Bert   I ain't saying I can. I ain't no psychic: like I give a shit about the noise out there and seeing through some fucken piece o' shit wall.

Raymond   No, sick, not *psychic*: *sick*. You're sick, Kowalski.

Bert   (*walking away*)   There's only one *sicko* in here and it ain't me.

Bert, *the bottle in his hand, moves to the door and looks out. He goes out and closes the door behind him. He flies back in through the door, falling on his backside, managing to keep the bottle upright.*

Voice (*off*): You just stay in there, shorty!

Bert *gets up and bangs on the door. It's locked.*

Bert   COCKSUCKER! You lousy fucken . . . (*Turns to* **Raymond**.) They've locked us in!

Raymond   What? You're insane, they can't . . .

He moves across to the door and tries it. It is locked. He bangs on it.

Please open this door. This door should *not* be locked from the outside. There are fire regulations posted on the wall of every corridor that clearly state this.

Bert *springs forward in panic and starts pounding the door.*

Bert   They're gonna torch this fucken joint with all us fucken midgets in it! They're gonna – it's a trick! They're gonna burn us all alive and make some big claim against one o' those insurance companies!

Raymond   Calm down. Will you calm down, you hysterical fool!

Bert *stops and takes a deep breath.*

Bert   You're right . . . I heard LeRoy telling Leo Singer that we were gonna all be needed a few more days . . .

The noises outside recede as **Raymond** *moves away from the door.*

Raymond   I'm calling the desk about this outrage! I'll demand that they put me on to Mervyn. He'll get to the bottom this nonsense, and heads *will* roll! Of that I can assure you.

He climbs up to the phone. He picks it up.

It's off the hook. They've left the phone off the hook!

Now very angry, he jumps down and paces around. He pounds the door violently.

I demand that you open this door immediately! I am a personal friend of Mervyn LeRoy!

Bert *looks at him.*

Bert   Forget it, Ray.

Raymond   How can I – How can I *forget* it, Kowalski? How can I *forget* that we're locked in here?

He picks up empty bottles of whisky, checking for dregs.

This is outrageous. Utterly outrageous.

Bert   You ain't wrong.

Raymond *lifts up his barbells from under his bed and starts doing arm curls in an increasingly demented rage.*

Bert *puts his ear to the door.*

Bert   I can hear noises . . . I think . . . yeah, I think somebody's coming.

He stands back as the door opens and **Philomena** *is pushed in. It slams shut behind her and is locked.* **Raymond** *puts the barbells on the bed.*

Bert   What the fuck?

Philomena   *Jaysus* . . .

Raymond   What is it, Miss Kinsella? What was all that noise? Why have they locked that damn door again?

Bert *tries to open it and bangs on it.*

Bert   Open the fucken door! (*Turns to* **Raymond**.) This ain't right.

Bert *takes a swig on the whisky. He shakes his head solemnly, looks down at the floor.*

Raymond   What the hell is going on here, Miss Kinsella? What was all the damn *commotion* about? We're locked in here; the regulations, the *fire* regulations have been blatantly flouted . . .

Philomena   . . . it was . . . it was . . .

She breaks down and runs sobbing into his arms. He is uncomfortable but sits her down next to him on the bed.

Raymond   Try to calm yourself, Miss Kinsella, try to calm yourself and speak. Take deep breaths . . . there . . . that's better . . .

Philomena *starts to compose herself a little.*

Philomena   . . . they were shooting a scene with Miss Garland and the others . . . they're shooting this *big* dance-number scene and – *Jaysus* – poor Charles, my poor angel . . . .

Raymond   Never mind that for now. You were out there. You . . . will you tell me what they're talking about in the corridor, and why are they keeping us locked in here?

Philomena   I need to . . . it's about the scene. The big . . . the big scene.

Bert   This is the big scene, right? Garland, the fucken Scarecrow, Cowardly Lion, the other one –

Raymond   Tin Man? Tin Woodsman?

Bert   Yeah, yeah, Tin Man.

Raymond   Jack Haley?

Bert   Whoever, you fucken *listening* to her?

Raymond   Yes, go on, Philomena: this big *scene* . . .
and . . . ?

Philomena   And this big scene they're shooting, all of a
sudden a Munchkin – oh Holy Mary, mother of God! Poor
Charles, my sweet angel . . .

Raymond   What? What about a Munchkin, Miss
Kinsella?.

Philomena   Mr Taylor . . . Mr Taylor, he said it was
Charles.

Raymond   What was Charles for heaven's sake? *What* was
Charles?

Philomena   . . . he's . . . Charles has . . . they're saying,
Jaysus, they're saying . . . there's a rumour, there's talk,
they're saying he's . . . saying he's hung himself from a tree.
Charles, our little Charlie. They're saying –

Raymond   What!

He turns away, clasping his face in shock, as **Bert** *puts an arm around
a wailing* **Philomena**. **Raymond** *turns round and looks at her
again.*

What did you say?

Bert   You heard her fine, Ray. Don't make her say it again,
OK?

Raymond   . . . This . . . this is what they're saying? They're
saying this out in the corridor? Charles has . . . *suicide*? Suicide
right out there – in front – out on the sound stage he's
committed –

Philomena   Not just in the corridor, they're saying it all
over the place.

Bert   Poor fucken kid. Knew he was close to the edge. Didn't realise *how* close.

He looks pointedly at **Raymond**, *who is visibly disturbed. He gets up and paces around.*

Raymond   . . . So . . . so they're saying a Munchkin . . . Charles, Charles has hung himself from a tree, from a tree on the sound stage?

Philomena   . . . Sure it was Charles, our little Charlie; Charles Merryweather, he was the Munchkin that hung himself . . .

Raymond   I don't believe it.

Bert   Tiny Taylor always gets his facts *right*. Tiny Taylor's great with facts. I believe it. Shit, why shouldn't I? The mess Charlie was in it makes sense he'd do something like that.

Raymond   And he says it's *Charles*? . . . Let me get this *straight.* He's saying Charles, *our* Charles has hung himself on the sound stage in front of –

Philomena   Yes! My poor, sweet Charlie. (*Pulls away from* **Bert**.) My angel. Corrupted by the evil around him!

She runs to the door, banging on it, then falling on her knees, pleading.

Let me out! I shouldn't be here! It was a mistake . . . (*Sobbing.*) Please, let me out. (*Turns back to* **Bert**.) You killed him, Kowalski! You killed him with your unholy ways, just as surely as if you'd shot him with a gun!

Raymond   A sentiment *I* heartily endorse, Miss Kinsella. (*To* **Bert**.) You've been the bad apple in the barrel right from the start, Kowalski.

Bert   I was the best friend that kid ever had! He told me so himself! We were buddies, f'chrissakes!

Raymond   You have *blood* on your hands, Kowalski, *blood*, but in a sense I blame myself. I ought to have nipped your malign influence on him in the bud straight away.

Bert *registers the blood on the floor again, he touches it, raises his hand. He looks to **Philomena**, then to **Raymond**, who falls silent. He then starts to look through **Charles**'s drawer. He finds the soiled diaper.*

Bert   . . . Christ!

Raymond *looks across.*

Raymond   . . . What's . . . what's that?

Raymond *goes over to **Bert**, who is staring at the bloody diaper.*

Bert   . . . Charlie's fucken diaper. It's . . .

Raymond *walks away and scouts the empty whisky bottles.*

Raymond   . . . I need – really I need a drink.

Bert *stares hard at the bloody diaper. Something has dawned on him. He looks at **Raymond**.*

Bert   . . . You – fucken – you've been . . .

*He shoots over to **Raymond** and shoves the diaper in his face. **Philomena** looks up and pulls herself to her feet.*

Raymond   Get – what're you –

Bert   Up to your old tricks, eh, Ray!

Raymond   Get that thing out of my face!

Bert   You – should o' known, should o' fucken known. What am I here, a fucken schmuck?

Raymond   You're insane!

Bert   This – it explains – this explains it all, you piece o' shit.

Raymond *cuts away from **Bert**, who angrily follows him around the room. **Raymond** is nervously on the back foot as Bert taunts him with the bloody diaper.*

Raymond   I'm warning you, stop waving that *thing* in my face.

Philomena *rises to her feet.*

Philomena   What in the name of Jaysus is going on here?

Bert   Old habits die hard, uh, Ray?

Raymond   If you're – you're sick if you're *insinuating* that I've anything to do with this, Kowalski.

Bert   You can't keep that dick o' yours out of assholes, can you, Ray?

Raymond   I could have have you – *slander*! It's slanderous what you're –

Bert   It ain't slander, Ray. It ain't fucken slander. It's *sodomy*, Ray. Fucken sodomy, that's what it is.

Philomena   What are you saying now, Bert Kowalski, you vile little man!

Raymond   He's lost his mind. (*To* **Bert**.) All those *drugs* – you've lost your mind, do you hear!

Raymond *tears the diaper from* **Bert**'s *hand and hurls it out the window. There is silence.*

Philomena   It was Charlie's diaper. I told him to see a doctor, about his back passage. It was bleeding.

Bert   Looks like he saw Doctor Ray here!

Philomena *looks at* **Raymond** *doubtfully.*

Philomena   I'm sure Raymond . . . Mr Benedict-Porter, wouldn't . . .

She steps back from **Raymond**.

Raymond   I only wanted –

Bert   I know what you wanted, Ray . . . Ray?

Raymond   What?

Bert   I know what you wanted. You wanted to take advantage, Ray. I know all about you.

Raymond   What's that supposed to mean?

Bert   Supposed to mean? It ain't 'supposed' to mean anything. It *means* I got your card marked, OK, Ray?

Raymond *pauses, turns and looks over at* **Bert**.

Raymond   . . . I never . . . suicide . . . there was just no need for it.

Bert   They'll investigate.

Raymond   They don't investigate suicide.

Bert   Not what it *was*, Ray, the *cause* of it. They'll investigate the *cause*, Ray.

Raymond   I should think –

Bert   You know what they're calling this place, Ray? Uh, Ray, uh? . . . Philomena? I'll tell you anyway: Babylon Heights. They're calling this place Babylon Heights, Ray. Police gonna come here and . . . not hard to imagine, right? They see a bunch o' little freaks and they put two and two together. Charlie . . . that's what I'm thinking. They won't just wanna know the *how*, Ray. They'll wanna know the *why*.

Raymond   Oh dear.

Bert   Yeah, exactly: *oh* fucken *dear*.

Bert *goes to his bag and pulls out his pipe.*

Raymond   Jesus Christ, Kowalski! How can you even think about smoking that stuff at a time like *this*?

Bert *stuffs the paraphernalia in his pillowcase.*

Philomena   Why did he go and do that? He was a good boy, even though he wasn't really like a boy. He was so gentle.

Raymond   Look, let's try to be rational. The deal here is –

Bert   Deal? You don't know how to *deal*. I know blind
pissants *deal* better than you, Ray. *Deal?* You ain't no fucken
gambler, Ray. You're a fucken calculator. Face it.

Raymond   *Calculator?*

Bert   That's right: you *calculate.*

Raymond   Whatever, whatever arrangement we –

Bert   Deals, arrangements, fucken treaties n' pacts, gimme
a blind pissant sonofabitch New Jersey landlord over your
calculating shit any day.

Raymond   Look –

Bert   Look? No: you look, *you* look, Raymond. I can handle
a fucken snoopy Keystone grilling me over my medicine but
what you caused here ain't no fucken joke, you hear me?

Raymond   I didn't – I'm not saying it is, Bert.

Bert   You shouldn't.

Raymond   I'm *not.* Look –

Bert   This ass aint for sale.

Raymond   I know, I –

Bert   You ain't gonna stick some fucken flag in my ass n'
claim it . . .

Raymond   I can produce some cash.

Philomena *is now interested.*

Bert   You're Mr Mervyn *LeRoy* now, you fucken – I can
produce my *ass* you can *produce.*

Raymond   If you'd just –

Bert   You don't produce shit, Ray . . . Ray?

Raymond   . . . What?

Bert   You don't produce shit, Ray, what you produce, Ray, is raggedy assholes and fucked-up insides with that big fucken dick o' yours.

Raymond   Please, please will you . . . *look*, Bert . . .

Bert   I seen dead panhandlers produce more n' you, you lying fairy ass cocksucker.

Raymond   This is going nowhere.

Bert   I don't agree, I think this is going *somewhere*. I think this might be leading to some ass fucker getting some hard labour when the Keystones start lookin to explain as to why they got a dead midget on a film set.

Philomena   Or a dope fiend.

Raymond   Exactly, Miss Kinsella –

Philomena   The pair of yis. The pair of yis killed my Charles. I should tell them all about your opium (*turns to* **Bert**, *then* **Raymond**) and your unnatural ways. Ruined that boy. My poor Charles . . .

Bert   Since when did he become *your* fucken Charles? His name was Charlie Fucken Merryweather. Since when did he become Charlie Fucken Baby-Leprechaun Kinsella?

Philomena   Since I was the only one that really cared for him! To you he was just a drinking partner in crime. (*Turns to* **Raymond**.) And to you he was just a toy to satisfy your evil, warped urges. How could you, Mr Benedict-Porter? He respected you! And I'm ashamed, ashamed is what I am, to say that I did too!

Raymond   Look, I –

Philomena   My poor, poor Charles. Oh, don't you worry; I'll be silent. I'll say nothing, cos it won't bring my poor Charles back now, will it? But sure, you'll pay for my silence, so yis will!

Bert   What the fuck are you sayin?

Philomena   I'm sayin that it's going to cost the both of you!

There is a long silence, which **Bert** *breaks with a loud laugh.*

Bert   It's gonna cost us! How much is it gonna cost us? You are one mean fucker. You are one mean, twisted, little bag of Paddy leprechaun shit! How much is it gonna fucken cost us?

Philomena   I want twenty-five dollars each, and I'll thank you to keep a civil tongue in your head, you poisonous little Polack bastard!

Bert *is dumbfounded for a beat; horrified but also somewhat impressed.*

Bert   I can't lay my hands on that kind of dough.

She turns to a sheepish **Raymond**.

Raymond   I can.

Philomena   Then I need fifty from you, Raymond. Fifty, or I'll tell them all about what you did to Charles.

Raymond   Fifty dollars and it stays in this room?

Philomena *nods cagily at him.*

Bert (*to* **Raymond**)   Whaaat! You been bumming whisky off me last three weeks n' now you can get your hands on fifty fucking bucks?

Raymond   . . . I . . . I won it, I won it if you must know.

Bert   *Shit.*

Raymond   Yes.

Bert   You won it? You don't *gamble*, Ray.

Raymond   I do.

Bert   You don't.

Raymond   . . . *Chess*, if you must know, I won it from poor Charles.

Pause.

Bert   You're shitting me, you cocksucker.

Raymond   I am not.

Bert   Shitting me big time; chess my hairy midget ass.

Pause.

Raymond   . . . All right, all right, if you want to know the truth –

Bert   I do, that's what I'm saying. I wanna know where you got it. Chess my ass. I reckon you fucken stole it – stole it from Charlie.

Raymond   No! I never took his money!

Philomena   I wouldn't be surprised.

Bert   That's it, ain't it! You not only fucked him in the ass, you stole the kid's money.

Raymond   All right, if you want to – look, it's an advance. Mervyn – Mr LeRoy gave me an advance on my wages.

A pause. **Bert** *is thinking. So is* **Philomena**. **Raymond** *staggers to his case under the bed, rummages around and takes out the dollar bills.* **Philomena** *pulls them out of his hands and starts counting them.*

Philomena   . . . That's fifty dollars! Is it Charlie's money?

Raymond   No, it's *my* money.

Bert   Bullshit.

Philomena   If it *is* Charlie's money . . .

Raymond   I swear that it isn't. Check with Mr LeRoy if you like.

Philomena   If it *is* his money . . . sure, he'd want *me* to have it before *you* . . .

Raymond   I'm positive he would, assuming it *was* his, but it's not, it's –

Philomena   I'm not a fool, Raymond. Don't take me for one.

Raymond   No. Of course not.

Bert   You're a fucken devious little witch, is what you are. No, honey, we're the fucken fools. (*Turns to* **Raymond**.) Specially you, Ray. Your ass is far too close to the ground for all that cocksuckin Ivy League bullshit you come out with. (*Turns to* **Philomena**.) But *you*; you got me, you got me fucken speechless and that don't happen often.

He shakes his head regarding **Philomena** *in a loathing admiration and starts preparing his pipe.*

Philomena   You call me all the names you like, Kowalski, but it's youse two who are the baddies! I did nothing wrong to Charlie. I tried to help him.

Bert   It's as well it's you that she cleaned out, Ray. My conscience is like my fucken wallet, as clean as a whistle. (*Turns to* **Philomena**.) If anyone killed Charlie, it's Mr Ass-fuck Arizona here!

Raymond *strikes* **Bert** *about the head as he about to light the pipe. Opium flakes spill from it on to the bed.*

Bert   Whoa, whoa – quit it!

Raymond   I've had it with you, Kowalski; had it with you and your bitter, poisonous mouth –

Bert   Leave me the fuck alone!

Bert *picks up the yellow brick and batters* **Raymond** *in the face with it.* **Raymond** *flails about and screams.* **Bert** *picks up an empty whisky bottle and brings it down hard on* **Raymond**'s *head. Raymond staggers across the room in blind panic. He knocks over* **Philomena**'s *make-up box before falling to the floor.* **Bert** *stands over him, the broken bottle in his hand.*

Raymond (*hysterical*)   . . . What're you –

Bert   Fuck *you*, fuck you, you midget fucking piece o' shit cocksucker, OK!

Raymond *scampers away, trying to get to his feet.* **Bert** *kicks* **Raymond**. **Raymond** *curls up in a ball.* **Philomena** *sees her make-up box tipped over and runs urgently towards it.*

Bert   . . . Nobody – you don't fuck with my *dope*, OK? Nobody fucks with my *medicine*.

Raymond   My head!

Bert *sees* **Philomena** *trying too quickly and furtively to tidy up the contents of the spilled box. He approaches her.*

Bert   What the fuck are you –

Philomena   Get back, it's my box, it's my –

Bert   But these ain't your cufflinks!

Raymond *gets up and bends down over the box, which is broken. It has a false bottom and there are several stolen items splayed out on the floor, including his cufflinks.*

Raymond   Why, you thieving . . .

Philomena *crosses herself and recites some Hail Marys.* **Bert** *reaches over and picks up a wallet that has fallen from the box. Inside it is a wad of cash.* **Philomena** *springs to her feet.* **Bert** *holds the money in the air as she tries to grab it from his outstretched hand.*

Bert   . . . the fuck is this, as if we didn't know already?

Philomena   That's my money! Give it here!

Bert   *You* took his goddam money!

Philomena   If you must know, I was given – I was given that money by several men in the crew for looking after them.

Bert   Yeah, sure. What the fuck is it doing in his wallet then? You took his fucken money!

Philomena   NO! I never did!

She throws a tantrum, falling down on the bed, punching the pillows with her fists, sobbing.

Bert   Stop that shit, it don't impress us.

She turns round and sits up, swinging her legs off the bed.

Philomena   I borrowed the wallet from him! He gave it to me to keep my money safe, he didn't want me losing it. We were close, me and Charlie, and I . . . I was looking after it for him.

Bert   Like you looked after Ray's cufflinks? You've been rumbled, you leprechaun cunt!

Raymond   We have a *criminal justice system* here in the United States of America, Miss Kinsella; a criminal justice system designed to protect *citizens of the United States of America*, like myself and Mr Kowalski, against foreign tricksters like yourself. These cufflinks have been in my family for three generations –

Philomena (*sobbing*)   I was only keeping them safe for you, I would have given them back . . .

Bert   You think you had it bad with them nuns back in Ireland; see how your little Irish ass likes it in prison with some of the dirtiest, nastiest broads this side of the pond, honey . . . right, Ray?

Raymond   The authorities will take a dim view of your behaviour, I can assure you, Miss Kinsella, a *dim view*. You will either be incarcerated here, as Mr Kowalski has suggested, or immediately deported home for punishment. This is a very serious matter.

Philomena *jumps on the spot in tearful frustration.*

Philomena   Oh Raymond, Bert, please . . . I know I've been bad, but we all have. It's this place . . . it's like poor Charlie says, it's evil. And now they've locked us in . . . what will become of us . . . ?

Raymond *and* **Bert** *look at each other.*

Philomena   And my poor, poor Charlie . . . us ruining each other won't bring him back, now will it? What's to be gained from it all? We . . . what we need to do is stick together.

Bert *thinks.* **Raymond** *stares at* **Philomena**.

Bert   She's right though, Ray, we're all to blame. We all gotta come clean here. And we *do* need to stick together now. We're locked up here, like you said, Ray, like fucken animals. It's us against those cocksuckers. Dwarfs don't have it easy, ever. Look how Charlie ended up, chrissakes.

Raymond   None of us are blameless, but we have to *remember* that Charles *did* take his own life.

Philomena   Which is a sin. (*Crosses herself, looking upwards.*) I'm sorry to speak ill of you, Charlie, but it is a sin to take the life that the Lord gave you.

Bert   But what a shitty life the poor little fucker had. What a fucken shitty *dwarf* life –

Raymond   Charles's problem wasn't his lack of inches. It was –

Philomena   The other thing?

Raymond   . . . his thin skin.

Bert (*to* **Philomena**)   What other thing? (*To* **Raymond**.) Whadaya mean, thin skin? The skin around his asshole?

Raymond   No! For heaven's sake, Kowalski, look outside. As bad as it is here, it's *worse* out there. People are struggling. Roosevelt's doing the best he can, but frankly . . . people are *struggling* to survive.

Bert   You don't need to tell me that, Ray. I been out there, you know. I gotta go back out there again . . . if these big pricks . . .

He launches at the door.

OPEN THIS FUCKEN DOOR!

He bangs on it hard again, but there is no response. He turns and looks to a sheepish **Philomena***.*

What other thing? What did you mean?

Raymond   Some of them, the thin-skinned ones, the born victims, they just go to the wall. And it doesn't matter what height you are; it's the stuff you are made of. If you are weak, then you will go down.

Bert   Sure you will, especially if you got a faggot rapist up your ass. (*To* **Philomena***.*) What other thing, dammit?

Philomena   Charles was an angel. He had none of the boy things. The bits that boy's have.

Bert   You mean he was a broad? You trying to tell me that Charlie was a fucken broad? You're fucken shittin! Charlie had a twat?

Philomena   I . . . Charles was . . . he was an angel.

Raymond   He was no angel, you stupid girl! My God, look at you, you thieving, whoring little ignoramus!

Philomena *looks briefly tearful, then screws her face up in a malicious defiance.* **Raymond** *shakes his head disdainfully.*

Raymond   You know from the circuses, Kowalski, you know about hermaphrodites. He was one of them. A commonplace occurrence in certain forms of dwarfism; incomplete or ill-formed sex organs.

Bert   Jesus . . . No wonder the poor little prick wasn't doing handstands when I told him about those Dutch broads. (*To* **Philomena***.*) How'd *you* know about it?

Philomena   He was sad, and I wanted to make him happy . . . (*shrugs casually*) the way you can make men happy.

Bert *looks to* **Raymond** *and they raise their eyebrows.*

Bert   Jeez, you were right, Ray. (*To* **Philomena***.*) I really underestimated you all along, Philomena. Poor Charlie. You stole his cash, then tried to suck a dick he didn't have.

Noise from offstage. The door is being unlocked.

Voice (*off*)   One of you guys, get your ass out here. We got a proposition t' make.

Bert and **Raymond** *both make a move.* **Philomena** *glares at them both.*

Voice (*off*)   Just one of ya!

They look at each other. **Bert** *nods at* **Raymond**, *and stands back.*

Bert   You're the fancy talker. Go ahead. Use your 'influence'.

Raymond *hesitates.* **Philomena** *nods at him and he tentatively exits. The door shuts behind him.*

Philomena   Where do you think they're taking him?

Bert   For a nice little fucken stroll down the yellow brick road with Mervyn LeRoy and the head of the cocksucking studio. How the fuck should I know?

Philomena   I only asked.

Bert   It ain't where they're takin him that's the big mystery to me, honey. The big mystery to me is where the hell did you learn to be such a devious little broad?

Philomena   I know I've sinned . . . but I've had to live that way, as God's my witness, it was the only way. I was living wild 'til the sisters took me in. I hated it there, I hated those nuns!

Bert   Yeah, it ain't no fun living with big people. And living with fucked-up broads who ain't getting their chimneys swept, I can only imagine how much that must stink. (*Pause.*) Bet they took it out on you, huh, kid?

Philomena   I was like a slave to those twisted, evil bitches. Sure I prayed every night to get out of that place. Then, when I was in town with Sister Bernadette one afternoon, I saw the advertisement for this production in our paper. Mr Singer had put it in. It seemed like the answer to all my prayers. So I stole the money from the convent and I headed out here.

Bert   I can't blame you for that, kid. But here it's different; here you gotta look after your own kind.

Philomena   I know I've done wrong, Mr Kowalski, but I pray all the time. I always ask for forgiveness for all my sins.

Bert   Jeez, I gotta do this religion thing; do what the fuck you like then just shoot off a quick prayer and your ass is clean again.

The door opens. **Raymond** *comes back in. The door shuts behind but is not locked.*

Raymond   They want to cut a deal.

Bert   The desk? The desk wants to cut a deal?

Philomena   What do they want?

Bert   Let's be clear about this, Ray, are we taking about the cocksucking desk or the fucken studio here?

Raymond   I was talking to the chap from the desk. I have absolutely no idea whom he is making the proposition on behalf of, Kowalski; hotel, production, studio, Culver City, or the US Government itself. Let's just say, and I'm sure that this will chime with your victim mentality, that the 'big people' have made us an offer.

Bert   Lousy cocksuck—

Raymond   Would you like to hear what this offer is?

Philomena   Yes, yes, tell us.

Pause.

Bert   Sure, go ahead.

Raymond   They want us to gather up all Charles's stuff into his suitcase and pass it out to them. If anyone asks, he left earlier today, saying that he planned to head back to London after doing some travelling.

Bert   That ain't no deal to me, Ray. That's half a fucken deal. The *wrong* fucken half.

Raymond   We are to be remunerated the sum of one hundred dollars each.

Philomena   One hundred dollars! Oh, we must take it. It's what poor Charles would have wanted us to do. My angel was too good for this world but he left us this good fortune!

Bert (*whistles*)   That's a lot o' dough for little people.

Raymond   I'm aware of that, Kowalski. We should . . . I don't know.

Bert   Mmmm.

Philomena   I say we take it!

She looks over to **Charles**'*s case, and falls down on to her knees in prayer.*

Raymond   It poses questions. Ethical questions.

Bert   Don't talk to me about tell me ethical questions. I don't need no lesson in 'ethical questions' from some hermwhatchamacallit fucking rapist, and (*turns to* **Philomena**) I sure as shit don't need no thieving cocksucking leprechaun Joan of Arc going all holy on my ass.

Philomena *scowls and rises.*

Raymond   Well? What do you think?

Bert   All I'm sayin is that it's a lot of dough and Charlie ain't comin back, poor little sucker.

Raymond   Quite. And whatever one says about the pressures that we, as actors on this production, have been under, whatever one's personal view of such pressures . . .

Bert   I know them pressures, Ray. Right, Philomena?

Philomena   With that money I could have my own little house here, with a nice big lock on the door.

Bert   Buys a fucken bolt-hole. Buys a stake in this midget community, for sure, and enough greenbacks to ride out the tough times.

Raymond   . . . there is the broader question of *loyalty*. As a friend of Mervyn LeRoy the disclosure right now of this act by Charles, this selfish act, of free will, and we would do well to remember that suicide is an act of free will . . . I suppose what I'm trying to say is that the negative publicity could jeopardise the entire production and for professional and personal reasons I'm loath to let that happen.

Bert   So you're gonna take one for the team, huh? You're so goddam noble, Ray. Saint fucken Ray. Of course, the hundred bucks means zilch to you.

Raymond   You've spoken at length about the importance of money, Kowalski. We're all fully aware of those ramifications.

Bert   Yes, I'm fully fucken aware. I ain't sayin this dumb Polack ass ain't for sale. But I've had it with the pious crap. And the one reason, the one good reason I can think of right now for taking that dough and getting out of this crummy joint, is that I won't ever have to listen to your bullshit no more!

He grabs **Charles**'s *case and lugs it towards the door. He bangs on the door.*

Open up, you lousy cocksuckin giraffe-assed freaks!

The door opens.

Go on, take it.

Bert *pushes the suitcase through the door and follows through after it, pursued by* **Philomena** *and* **Raymond**, *as 'Somewhere Over the Rainbow' starts to play in refrain.*